Collins

Health and Social Care

Level 2 Dementia Care Award and Certificate

Mark Walsh · Elaine Millar · John Rowe · Ann Mitchell

Published by Collins Education
An imprint of HarperCollins*Publishers*
77–85 Fulham Palace Road
Hammersmith
London
W6 8JB

Browse the complete Collins Education catalogue at
www.collinseducation.com

10 9 8 7 6 5 4 3 2 1

ISBN 978-0-00-746871-3

Mark Walsh, Elaine Millar, John Rowe and Ann Mitchell assert their moral rights
to be identified as the authors of this work.

British Library Cataloguing in Publication Data

A Catalogue record for this publication is available from the British Library.

Project managed by Caroline Low
Edited by Jan Doorly and Matthew Hammond
Index by Jane Coulter
Picture research by Matthew Hammond
Design and typesetting by Jouve India Private Ltd.
Illustrations by Ann Paganuzzi
Cover design by Angela English
Printed and bound in Italy by Lego

Contents

	Introduction	2

Chapter 1   **Understanding and caring for the individual**   **4**

DEM 201   Dementia awareness

DEM 202   The person-centred approach to the care and support of individuals with dementia

DEM 204   Understand and implement a person-centred approach to the care and support of individuals with dementia

Chapter 2   **Communication and interaction with individuals with dementia**   **52**

DEM 205   Understand the factors that can influence communication and interaction with individuals who have dementia

DEM 210   Understand and enable interaction and communication with individuals with dementia

Chapter 3   **Equality, diversity and inclusion in dementia care**   **80**

DEM 207   Understand equality, diversity and inclusion in dementia care

DEM 209   Equality, diversity and inclusion in dementia care practice

DEM 211   Approaches to enable rights and choices for individuals with dementia while minimising risks

Chapter 4   **The use of medication in dementia care**   **132**

DEM 305   Understand the administration of medication to individuals with dementia using a person-centred approach

HSC 3047   Support the use of medication in social care settings

Chapter 5   **The nutritional requirements of individuals with dementia**   **176**

DEM 302   Understand and meet the nutritional requirements of individuals with dementia

Resources   **206**

Index   **209**

Acknowledgements   **214**

Introduction

Welcome to the Health and Social Care Level 2 Dementia Care handbook!

Older people, particularly those over 80 years, are the fastest growing age group in the UK population. This group also has the highest risk of developing dementia-based conditions. You can develop dementia at any age, though the risk increases as you get older. About 20 per cent of people over the age of 80 years develop one form of dementia or another. This handbook isn't about dementia as an illness or a condition, though. It is about ways of caring for and supporting people living with dementia.

In the early stages of a dementia-based condition, some people can manage without outside help and are able to continue living at home. As the condition progresses, virtually all individuals with dementia require some level of care and support to cope with daily living. Individuals with dementia need to be cared for and supported by people who understand what is happening to them.

Health and social care workers who practice in dementia care settings or who provide dementia care and support in the community need to be able to use an empathetic, person-centred approach that focuses on the quality of life, dignity and personhood of individuals with dementia. This handbook emphasises the importance of treating every individual with dementia as a unique, valued adult in their own right, regardless of the way dementia affects them. It explains what a person-centred approach involves and what you need to do to demonstrate that you have the skills to work in a person-centred way.

How is the book organised?

The book consists of five chapters and a resources section.

▶ Each chapter of the book covers one or more of the units that make up the Level 2 Award in Awareness of Dementia Care or the Level 2 Certificate in Dementia Care.

▶ Each chapter is divided into different sections, which are matched to the specifications for the Level 2 qualifications. Each section provides you with a focused and manageable chunk of learning.

Overall, the chapters cover all of the learning and assessment requirements of the Level 2 Award and Certificate qualifications.

How is assessment covered?

In order to achieve your Level 2 Award, you will need to provide evidence of your knowledge and understanding of dementia care as well as your practical competence as a dementia care worker in a real work environment. Each chapter of this book ends with a checklist of 'What you need to know' and 'What you need to do' in order to successfully complete the units that a chapter covers. This checklist will help you keep track of your progress.

The suggested assessment tasks in each chapter will help you gather the evidence you need for each unit. Your tutor or assessor will help you to plan your work in order to meet the overall assessment requirements of your target qualification.

We hope that the material in this handbook is accessible, interesting and inspires you to pursue a rewarding career caring for and supporting individuals with dementia. Good luck with your course and your future career!

Mark Walsh, Elaine Millar, John Rowe and Ann Mitchell

Qualification information

The book has been written to cover the:

▶ Level 2 Award in Awareness of Dementia qualification
▶ Level 2 Certificate in Dementia Care qualification

The units that make up the Level 2 Award provide learners new to dementia care work or those preparing for employment in this area with a solid awareness of dementia care issues. The knowledge gained through the achievement of the Award qualification can also be used to demonstrate competence in the Level 2 Certificate in Dementia Care. This qualification is aimed at those who are already working in care roles with individuals with dementia. It provides learners with an opportunity to have their practical competence as dementia care workers assessed.

Level 2 Award in Awareness of Dementia

Learners aiming to achieve a Level 2 Award in Awareness of Dementia must complete and pass the four mandatory units listed below.

Unit code	Mandatory units	Credits	Book chapter
DEM 201	Dementia awareness	2	1
DEM 202	The person-centred approach to care and support of individuals with dementia	2	1
DEM 205	Understand the factors that can influence communication and interaction with individuals who have dementia	2	2
DEM 207	Understand equality, diversity and inclusion in dementia care	2	3

Level 2 Certificate in Dementia Care

Learners aiming to achieve a Level 2 Certificate in Dementia Care must complete and pass the five mandatory units and the three optional units listed below. (A range of additional optional units can also be taken to achieve the Level 2 Certificate, but are not covered by this handbook.)

Unit code	Mandatory units	Credits	Book chapter
DEM 201	Dementia awareness	2	1
DEM 204	Understand and implement a person-centred approach to the care and support of individuals with dementia	3	1
DEM 209	Equality, diversity and inclusion in dementia care practice	3	3
DEM 210	Understand and enable interaction and communication with individuals with dementia	3	2
DEM 211	Approaches to enable rights and choices for individuals with dementia while minimising risks	3	3
Unit code	Optional units	Credits	Book chapter
DEM 302	Understand and meet the nutritional requirements of individuals with dementia	3	5
DEM 305	Understand the administration of medication to individuals with dementia using a person-centred approach	3	4
HSC 3047	Support the use of medication in social care settings	5	4

The achievement of units from both the Award and the Certificate qualifications can be used towards the achievement of the Level 2 Diploma in Health and Social Care (Adults) for England or the Level 2 Diploma in Health and Social Care (Adults) for Wales and Northern Ireland.

1 | Understanding and caring for the individual

DEM 201
LO1 Understand what dementia is

- ▶ Explain what is meant by the term 'dementia'

- ▶ Describe the key functions of the brain that are affected by dementia

- ▶ Explain why depression, delirium and age-related memory impairment may be mistaken for dementia

DEM 201
LO2 Understand key features of the theoretical models of dementia

- ▶ Outline the medical model of dementia

- ▶ Outline the social model of dementia

- ▶ Explain why dementia should be viewed as a disability

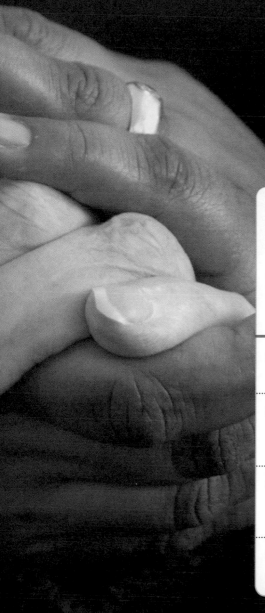

**DEM 201
LO3 Know the most common types of dementia and their causes**

- ▶ List the most common causes of dementia
- ▶ Describe the likely signs and symptoms of the most common causes of dementia
- ▶ Outline the risk factors for the most common causes of dementia
- ▶ Identify prevalence rates for different types of dementia

**DEM 201
LO4 Understand factors relating to an individual's experience of dementia**

- ▶ Describe how different individuals may experience living with dementia depending on age, type of dementia and level of ability and disability
- ▶ Outline the impact that the attitudes and behaviours of others may have on an individual with dementia

**DEM 202
LO1 Understand
approaches that
enable individuals
with dementia to
experience wellbeing**

▸ Describe what is meant by a
person-centred approach

▸ Outline the benefits of
working with an individual
with dementia in a person-
centred manner

**DEM 202
LO2 Understand the
role of carers in the
care and support
of individuals with
dementia**

▸ Describe the role that carers
can have in the care and
support of individuals with
dementia

▸ Explain the value of developing
a professional working
relationship with carers

**DEM 202
LO3 Understand the
roles of others in the
support of individuals
with dementia**

▸ Describe the roles of others
in the care and support of
individuals with dementia

▸ Explain when it may be
necessary to refer to others
when supporting individuals
with dementia

▸ Explain how to access the
additional support of others
when supporting individuals
with dementia

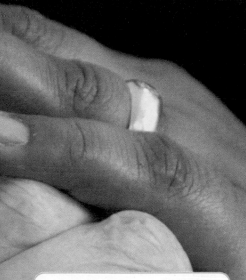

CHAPTER 1

DEM 204
LO1 Understand the importance of a person-centred approach to dementia care and support

▶ Describe what is meant by a person-centred approach

▶ Describe how a person-centred approach enables individuals with dementia to be involved in their own care and support

DEM 204
LO2 Be able to involve the individual with dementia in planning and implementing their care and support using a person-centred approach

▶ Explain how information about personality and life history can be used to support an individual to live well with dementia

▶ Communicate with an individual with dementia using a range of methods that meet individuals' abilities and needs

▶ Involve an individual with dementia in identifying and managing risks for their care and support plan

▶ Involve an individual with dementia in opportunities that meet their agreed abilities, needs and preferences

DEM 204
LO3 Be able to involve carers and others in the care and support of individuals with dementia

▶ Explain how to increase a carer's understanding of dementia and a person-centred approach

▶ Demonstrate how to involve carers and others in the support of an individual with dementia

What is dementia?

Introduction to this chapter

This chapter focuses on the knowledge and skills you need to address a range of basic dementia awareness and communication-related issues in dementia care practice. The chapter covers everything you need to know to complete three closely related units of the level 2 Dementia Care Award and Certificate: DEM 201, DEM 202 and DEM 204.

Your assessment criteria:

DEM 201

1.1 Explain what is meant by the term 'dementia'.

🔑 **Key term**

Dementia: a progressive long-term condition that affects the functioning of the brain leading to memory loss

What is dementia?

Dementia is a long-term condition that normally affects people aged 65 and older. However, younger people can also be affected. It is a progressive condition that leads to loss of key functions of the brain. Dementia is predicted to become more common as a result of the ageing population of the UK.

Dementia covers a range of symptoms which interfere with an individual's ability to function normally. These include:

- loss of memory
- confusion
- speech and language problems
- loss of ability to make sound judgment
- loss of concentration
- difficulty in processing information
- changes in personality and behaviour.

Generally, an individual will need to exhibit the above symptoms for at least six months before positive diagnoses of dementia can be made.

Initially, the person may seem grumpy, appear withdrawn, and will tend to opt out of social activities. As the condition progresses, they may experience difficulties with time, with not knowing the day of the week, the date of the month or even what year it is. Gradually, a person with dementia may go on to develop problems identifying friends, key family members and eventually themselves. They can become disoriented, and frequently fail to recognise their surroundings. They may also experience difficulties communicating emotions, remembering how to do everyday things and recalling specific events. Dementia is progressive: the person's ability to function deteriorates over a period of time.

Investigate

Using the internet, your local library and other resources, conduct further research into the symptoms of dementia.

Case study

George is 70 years old. He lives with his daughter and grandson in Scotland. He is an active man who plays bowls three times a week and belongs to a group of ramblers. His daughter has noticed that George is becoming forgetful and gets very frustrated when he cannot remember simple things like how to boil an egg. He also becomes quite aggressive when she tries to help.

1. What symptoms is George exhibiting?

2. What would you do in order to find out more about George's problem?

3. How can you help his daughter understand George's problem?

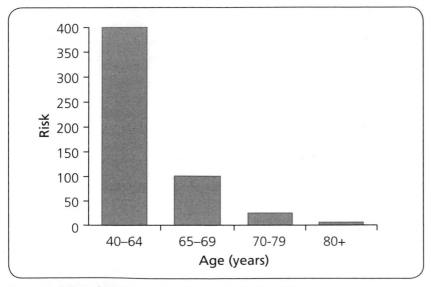

Figure 1.1 Prevalence rates for dementia in the UK

? | Reflect

Think about a recent conversation you have had with an individual with a dementia-related condition in your work or placement setting. What symptoms did this individual exhibit that made you consider that the cause was dementia?

How does dementia affect the brain?

How dementia affects the brain

The Alzheimer's Society (2010) states that the brain consists of three main sections: the **hindbrain**, **midbrain** and the **forebrain**. Each section of the brain is responsible for controlling specific physical or mental functions. The hindbrain and midbrain are concerned with basic life support functions such as blood pressure and respiration. The forebrain is concerned with memory and language, and is further divided into four sections: the frontal, parietal, occipital and temporal lobes (see figure 1.2).

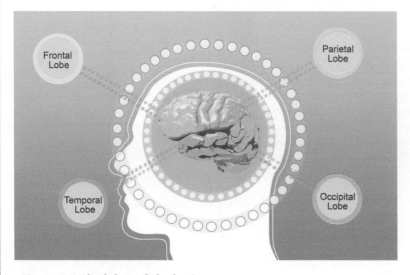

Figure 1.2 The lobes of the brain

The forebrain is the section of the brain affected by dementia. The Alzheimer's Society is very clear as to how each lobe is affected by the onset of dementia:

• The frontal lobe enables the individual to plan actions and learn new tasks. If there are problems with this lobe, the individual has to relearn certain routine tasks affected by dementia. These tasks may include shopping or cooking.

• The parietal lobe provides the individual with information about **spatial** relationships and **perception**. If the parietal lobe is damaged, the individual's ability to recognise objects, people or surroundings can be severely affected. This is why a person with dementia may sometimes fail to recognise a familiar face.

Your assessment criteria:

DEM 201

1.2 Describe the key functions of the brain that are affected by dementia.

Key terms

Forebrain: this part of the brain is concerned with receiving and processing information

Hindbrain: this part of the brain regulates essential functions such as breathing, swallowing, blood circulation and maintaining balance

Midbrain: regulates vision, hearing and body movement

Perception: is a process by which a person detects and interprets information from within the environment

Spatial: refers to general awareness of your immediate surroundings

- The occipital lobe deals with visual information. An individual affected by dementia may consequently have difficulty *seeing* what an object is, despite having reasonable eyesight or wearing a visual aid such as spectacles.

- The temporal lobe is focused on memory and language. Short-term memory, or memory for recent events, is often impaired in individuals with dementia. Recalling the day's events, therefore, is much more difficult than remembering childhood or distant memories, which are more deeply stored, and thus less affected by dementia. The ability to describe, explain, sequence thoughts and to think logically is also affected by damage to the temporal lobe.

? Reflect

Can you think of anybody you know well who has experienced the symptoms of a dementia-related disease? Which aspects of their functioning were affected? Can you link their symptoms to changes in one of the four lobes of the forebrain?

Case study

Victor is a 79 year old man who lives on his own. He has lived an active life; since his retirement he has looked after his personal needs, prepared his own meals and most days had a cup of tea and cake with his neighbour Miriam. About six months ago, Miriam noticed a change in Victor's behaviour. He no longer goes shopping like he used to and seems to have lost his cooking skills. He mainly eats meat pies and biscuits. On occasions Victor seems to forget where he is or does not recognise Miriam. He has also complained of not seeing very well when trying to read his newspapers, even though he has recently had his eyes tested and has been using his new glasses.

1. What signs or symptoms suggest that Victor has a dementia-related disease?

2. Which sections of Victor's brain are likely to be affected by the dementia-related disease?

3. How is dementia affecting Victor's everyday living skills?

Depression, delirium and age-related memory impairment

Depression, delirium and age-related memory impairment are sometimes mistaken for dementia. This is because these conditions can have a similar effect on a person's behaviour and communication skills as a dementia-related condition. As a result, it is important to know about and be able to compare the symptoms of depression, delirium and age-related memory loss with those of dementia. This makes understanding the difference between dementia and these other conditions much easier.

Depression

Depression and dementia share a number of symptoms, including:

- low motivation

- apathy

- memory problems

- slow speech

- slow movements.

Similarities between the symptoms of dementia and depression can make a diagnosis of dementia difficult. However, there are some key differences between the symptoms of the two conditions. The symptoms of depression, for example, include:

- rapid mental decline

- slow speech or movement

- a negative view on life.

These symptoms are not features of dementia, but may co-exist with the symptoms of dementia if the person has dementia and is also depressed. Symptoms of dementia that are not a feature of depression include:

- slow mental decline

- loss of touch with familiar surroundings

- progressive confusion and disorientation

- impaired motor skills, and loss of the ability to write, read and even speak

Your assessment criteria:

DEM 201

 1.3 Explain why depression, delirium and age-related memory impairment may be mistaken for dementia.

Key terms

Cognitive impairment: *loss of ability to think, concentrate and remember information*

Delirium: *sudden, severe confusion and rapid changes in brain function that occur with physical or mental illness. Delirium is also described as an acute toxic confusional state*

Depression: *a mood disorder characterised by intense sadness that disrupts an individual's daily life*

Memory impairment: *a part of the normal ageing process characterised by episodes of forgetfulness*

- short-term memory loss

- problems with time.

A person with dementia may try to cover up their memory loss, either by making excuses for their forgetfulness, confusion or other symptoms or by hiding their difficulties from acquaintances, friends and family. The condition tends to be progressive: it worsens rather than improves over time. In contrast, depression is treatable with medication, responds well to talking therapies like counselling, and will often improve even without the help of drugs or talking therapies.

Delirium

A person with delirium can suffer a form of **cognitive impairment** similar to that affecting someone with dementia. Delirium is also known as acute confusion, and is caused by illness or drug toxicity. Delirium is diagnosed by the following symptoms:

- mental incoherence

- difficulty in maintaining concentration and attention

- unconsciousness.

With dementia, a person's concentration may be severely reduced and there is a great deal of mental confusion, but they are not unconscious. Another difference between the two conditions is that delirium is often reversible because it can be treated and cured. Dementia, however, is irreversible and cannot be cured.

Age-related memory impairment

Age-related memory impairment is not easy to distinguish from dementia. This causes a lot of anxiety for some older people who are fearful of developing dementia. As we have seen, memory loss is a significant aspect of dementia. However, memory impairment is also an accepted result of the ageing process. A naturally occurring, age-related decline in the brain's cognitive function means that as people age they will inevitably find remembering things more difficult. The naming of people, places and things is especially affected by age-related memory impairment.

However, intellectual brain function remains intact and, while unable to name them, a person with age-related memory impairment will continue to recognise people, places and objects, and will not experience the depth of memory loss experienced by a person with dementia.

? | Reflect

What do you see as the main differences between age-related memory impairment and dementia?

Case study

Mimi is an 85-year-old woman who has been admitted to a ward in a hospital trust. On admission, Mimi was tearful but she couldn't explain why. Her clothes were dirty and she just wanted to lie in bed and sleep. In the two days since her admission, Mimi's appetite has been poor, even though (according to her son) she normally eats well.

Mimi does not seem to know where she is at the moment, even though members of staff have told her on several occasions that she is in hospital. Mimi's admission notes say that she did not recognise her son when he visited her at home and found her in this tearful, dirty and confused state. It was her son who called her GP. The GP then referred her to hospital for admission and assessment.

1. Identify three signs or symptoms that suggest Mimi may be mentally unwell.

2. Why might a relative or neighbour think that Mimi has a dementia-related illness?

3. What do you think could be wrong with Mimi?

 Discuss

Discuss with colleagues why depression and age-related memory impairment are mistaken for dementia.

Knowledge Assessment Task

This assessment task covers DEM 201 1.1, 1.2, 1.3.

Maureen Jacobs is 78 years of age. She is in good physical health and lives an active lifestyle. Maureen's daughter, Jenny, has noticed that her mum has started to become forgetful and sometimes gets confused when Jenny takes her shopping to the local supermarket. Maureen has laughed this off as 'having a senior moment' but Jenny thinks there may be more to it.

Maureen doesn't want to go to see her GP about her forgetfulness and Jenny accepts this. However, Jenny is keen to find out more about mental health conditions that can affect people in later life. You have been asked to produce information for Jenny that:

1. *explains what the term 'dementia' means*

2. *describes the key functions of the brain that are affected by dementia*

3. *explains why depression, delirium and age-related memory impairment are sometimes mistaken for dementia.*

You should keep the work that you produce as evidence towards your assessment.

Theoretical models of dementia

In the context of health and social care, **models** are ways of thinking about, understanding and responding to health and care related issues. Models of health and illness also enable practitioners to develop practical ways of caring for people. In this section, we will examine three theoretical models considered suitable for working with individuals with dementia. These are known as the:

- medical model
- social model
- dementia as a disability model.

Medical model of dementia

Practitioners who use a medical model view dementia as an incurable physical illness. The priorities of practitioners who use a medical model approach are to:

- identify signs and symptoms of brain disease so that a diagnosis can be given
- prescribe drugs considered appropriate for treating the symptoms of dementia.

The medical model approach to dementia focuses on the physical changes in the person's brain and on finding treatments that slow these changes down and improve a person's ability to function.

Your assessment criteria:

DEM 201

2.1 Outline the medical model of dementia.

2.2 Outline the social model of dementia.

2.3 Explain why dementia should be viewed as a disability.

Key term

Models: *ways of thinking about, describing or explaining something*

Discuss

Observe the care you see being given to individuals with dementia in a care home or in your placement setting. Discuss whether or not a medical model is being used to inform and deliver this care.

However, many in health and social care see limitations in the medical model of dementia. They argue that focusing on prescribing drugs as the main form of treatment devalues the individual, and that people are disempowered and further disabled by the process of becoming 'dementia patients'. Some health and social care practitioners also claim that those who use a medical model approach tend to dismiss the effectiveness of other models of care for people living with dementia.

Social model of dementia

The social model of dementia encourages care practitioners to focus on understanding the individual's experiences of living with dementia and on ways of enabling people to maintain their daily living skills. The social model places an emphasis on carers building a relationship with the individual and on maintaining a positive, supportive social environment for the person living with dementia. This is because a well-structured social network and an appropriate living environment, supported by carers with an understanding of dementia, can help individuals with dementia to help themselves in many ways. The social model of dementia attempts to provide individuals with the necessary tools with which to manage the effects of their condition for as long as possible.

? **Reflect**

What do you see as the main differences between the social and medical models of dementia? Do you know of any care providers or services using a social model to provide support and care for people with dementia-related conditions?

Dementia as a disability

The dementia as a disability model uses the concept of **disability** to help people:

- understand the disabling impact of dementia

- identify how they can learn to cope with their condition as 'disabled people'.

The dementia as a disability model is person centred, as it focuses on the particular effects of an individual's dementia on their ability to function, and on developing ways in which they can adapt to and overcome the problems they face within their own life. The model helps individuals to manage their dementia from the start and continues to help them adapt to new problems as the condition develops. Health and social care practitioners who use this model suggest that it:

- gives dignity back to the individual with dementia

- promotes and protects the rights of individuals with dementia

- ensures that a **needs-led assessment** is carried out when an individual is first diagnosed with dementia.

A needs-led assessment that identifies and takes into account an individual's strengths and abilities is an important part of this approach. This type of assessment enables an individual and their carers to make decisions about the kinds of care and support that are required and which are best suited to the individual. Health and social care practitioners who adopt a dementia as disability approach would argue that where a person can manage their own daily living needs, perhaps with a suitable level of community care support, they should remain living in their own home for as long as possible. Inpatient care is only considered when a person can no longer be supported at home and requires **safeguarding** against risks associated with later stages of dementia (see figure 1.3).

A person's care needs will increase as their dementia progresses. As this happens, a person's mental capacity is affected to the point where they may require the assistance of an **advocate** and protection from the **Mental Capacity Act 2005**. Among other things, the Mental Capacity Act ensures that the incapacitated individual is provided with an advocate.

 Discuss

Do you know any older people who do not have dementia but who worry that their memory and thinking abilities are fading? How could you reassure them about this? Share ideas with a work or class colleague.

 Key terms

Advocate: *a person who represents the views of another who is unable to do so*

Disability: *a limitation that prevents an individual from carrying out a certain task or action*

Mental Capacity Act 2005: *a law that protects the rights of people who cannot make decisions for themselves due to a learning disability or mental health condition, or for any other reason*

Needs-led assessment: *an assessment of an individual that focuses on their health and social care needs*

Safeguarding: *protecting from danger and harm*

Figure 1.3 Risks associated with later stages of dementia

An advocate is a person who is legally bound to act on behalf of the person they represent. For example, an advocate may have to make a decision about where the person they represent is cared for and what type of care services they receive. These are difficult decisions to make and an advocate must keep the person with dementia informed throughout the process.

? | Reflect

What do you see as the strengths and weaknesses of dementia as a disability model? Jot down some of your ideas, particularly relating to the value of a needs-led approach to assessment.

Case study

Beryl is now in the advanced stages of dementia. She was managing well at home with the help of two professional carers who visited twice a day and her niece Marion who lived nearby and often visited during the day. However, Marion recently noticed that her aunt had started to become aggressive and abusive towards her and was refusing to eat. Marion has withdrawn her services and now refuses to visit Beryl. The carers have also become concerned about the situation and, following discussion with Beryl, contacted Social Services. A care manager suggested that Beryl will need the protection of the Mental Capacity Act and an advocate to represent her interests as she does not have any other surviving relatives.

1. How could Beryl's care be managed using the medical model?

2. How would the social model improve the relationship between Beryl and her niece Marion?

3. How does the disability model enhance the care that is delivered to Beryl?

4. What would the advocate do for Beryl in this particular situation?

Knowledge Assessment Task

This assessment task covers DEM 201 2.1, 2.2, 2.3.

Barbara Davies-Hughes is the chairwoman of a *Women in Business* group in your local area. Barbara and her members meet every other Thursday to discuss business issues and find out about services in the local community. Your work setting has received a letter from Barbara asking whether somebody would be able to attend one of their meetings in a few weeks' time to tell them about different approaches to dementia and dementia care. Your manager is aware that you are studying for the Adult Diploma in Health and Social Care and has asked you to prepare some information for a talk on this. You have been asked to:

1. *outline the medical model of dementia*

2. *outline the social model of dementia*

3. *explain why dementia should be viewed as a disability.*

Keep a copy of the work that you produce for this activity as evidence towards your assessment.

Common types of dementia

Common causes, signs and symptoms of dementia based conditions

The term 'dementia' is used to describe a range of conditions that affect the brain and cognitive functioning. In reality, there are many causes of 'dementia'. The most common forms are:

- Alzheimer's disease
- Lewy body dementia
- Vascular dementia
- Frontotemporal dementia

Alzheimer's disease

Alzheimer's disease is one of the most common causes of dementia. It kills brain cells and nerves, causing changes in the chemistry and structure of the brain.

Gaps develop in the temporal lobe and in the **hippocampus**, both of which are responsible for storing and retrieving new information. These gaps affect the individual's ability to remember, speak, think and make decisions.

The Alzheimer's Society (2010) lists the following as signs and symptoms of Alzheimer's disease:

- lapses in memory, especially for recent events
- mood swings – busting into tears for no reason, for example
- forgetfulness of recent events
- personality changes
- wandering, particularly in the middle of the night
- getting lost
- loss of inhibitions – making inappropriate sexual advances, for example
- neglect of personal hygiene.

Alzheimer's disease accounts for between 50% and 60% of all cases of dementia (Alzheimer's Society, 2010).

Your assessment criteria:

DEM 201

3.1 List the most common causes of dementia.

3.2 Describe the likely signs and symptoms of the most common causes of dementia.

 Key terms

Alzheimer's disease: a disease that causes changes in the brain, affecting a person's speech, thoughts and communication

Frontotemporal dementia: also known as Pick's disease, it is caused by damage to the temporal lobe of the brain

Hippocampus: stores long-term memories of personal events

Lewy body dementia: a form of dementia caused by Lewy bodies, which have been likened to clumps of protein in the brain. The presence of these bodies damages brain cells, giving rise to dementia

Vascular dementia: a form of dementia resulting from the accumulative effect of a series of mini strokes, causing the brain cells to die

Lewy body dementia

Lewy body dementia is caused by the development of Lewy bodies inside the nerve cells. They disrupt the brain's capacity to function normally, leading to degeneration of brain tissue. This then gives rise to dementia. The signs and symptoms of Lewy body dementia are:

- memory loss

- persistent visual hallucinations – seeing things or people or animals that are not there

- problems with attention and alertness

- decline in problem-solving skills – for example, finding it difficult to plan ahead

- loss of facial expression

- confusion and delirium with nightmares

- propensity to faint or fall.

 Investigate

Using the internet, your library and other sources, find out the common causes of dementia based conditions and identify which part of the brain is affected for each cause.

 Reflect

Think about a conversation you have had with an individual who has had either Alzheimer's disease or Lewy body dementia. What were the signs and symptoms of that particular condition?

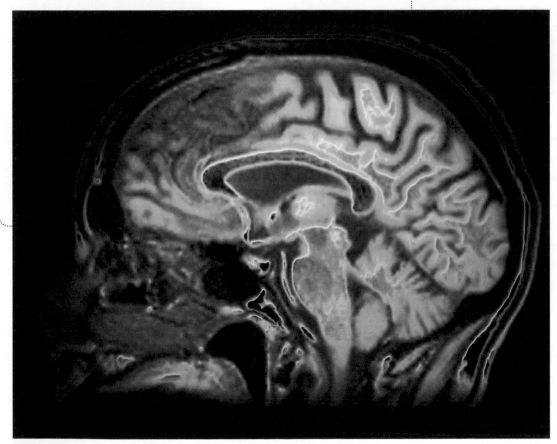

MRI scans of the brain can reveal dementia-related damage

Vascular dementia

Vascular dementia occurs when the blood vessels in the brain are damaged causing oxygen supply to be diminished. This can result in a series of mini strokes (infarcts), causing the brain cells to die.

Initially, the strokes will have either no symptoms, or simply leave the individual feeling confused. However, over a period of time, the cumulative effect of these mini strokes leads to vascular dementia.

The signs and symptoms of vascular dementia are:

- problems with communication and concentration
- stroke symptoms; for example, leg or arm weakness
- stepped progression – symptoms level off then condition deteriorates
- acute confusion
- memory loss
- dizziness
- slurred speech
- rapid shuffling steps
- loss of bladder and bowel control.

Frontotemporal dementia

Frontotemporal dementia consists of a range of conditions, including Pick's disease, frontal lobe degeneration and a type of dementia associated with motor neurone disease.

Frontotemporal dementia occurs as a result of damage to the frontal lobe or temporal parts of the brain, where there is an abnormal accumulation of proteins between the spaces of the cells. In the case of Pick's disease, these proteins are called Pick's bodies.

The signs and symptoms of frontotemporal dementia are:

- lack of insight
- an inability to empathise
- changing or inappropriate behaviour
- loss of inhibitions
- development of compulsive rituals
- increased interest in sex

Discuss

Have you ever provided care for individuals who were disinhibited or whose behaviour was socially inappropriate? Discuss what these people did and share ideas about how care workers could help to safeguard people who do this and protect their dignity.

Investigate

Use an internet search engine or reference books to find out about the causes and effects of 'strokes'. These are also known as cerebro-vascular accidents, so investigate this term too.

- agitated or blunted emotions

- a decline in personal hygiene

- language difficulties – not understanding the spoken word or failure to speak.

Investigate

Using online and library sources, investigate one of the four common forms of dementia further. Try to find out about ways of assessing and diagnosing your chosen form of dementia, its specific causes, and the impact it has on an individual's behaviour and functioning as the disease progresses.

Case study

Isobel is a 65-year-old lady who lives with her husband Gavin. She has led a very sociable and active life until a year ago when Gavin became increasingly concerned about his wife's short-term memory loss.

Isobel had a fall eight months ago and following the fall, Gavin noticed a change in his wife's behaviour. She became confused, started to ask the same questions over and over again and lost interest in her daily activities of cooking and cleaning the house. She also started hoarding things.

A few weeks later, she complained of feeling dizzy and sustained another fall that resulted in her having slurred speech and walking with rapid shuffling steps. Isobel has a history of hypertension and heart problems.

1. Identify what you think might be the cause of Isobel's problems.

2. What are the signs and symptoms of this condition?

3. Which part of the brain do you think is affected?

Knowledge Assessment Task

This assessment task covers DEM 201 3.1, 3.2.

The manager of your work setting has looked through the information you produced about dementia for the *Women in Business* group in a previous task (see page 17). She has suggested that the information could be extended a little to broaden the understanding of people attending the meeting. You have been asked to:

1. *list the most common causes of dementia*

2. *describe the likely signs and symptoms of the most common causes of dementia.*

You could add this information to the information leaflet or presentation notes that you have prepared for the previous task. Remember to keep your work so that you can use it as evidence towards your assessment.

Risk factors and prevalence rates

Risk factors

It is not understood exactly why some people develop dementia-related conditions, but there are certain **risk** factors that are associated with the condition. These are:

- age – people aged 65 years and older are at much higher risk of dementia

- family history – you are more likely to develop the illness if a close relative has been affected

- environmental and lifestyle factors – these include excess intake of alcohol, lack of exercise, exposure to aluminium and other metals, inappropriate diet

- head injury – a connection has been found between head injuries and dementia

- physical conditions – risk factors include hypertension, heart disease, HIV and multiple sclerosis

- genetics – risk factors include Down's syndrome

- learning disabilities.

Your assessment criteria

DEM 201

3.3 Outline the risk factors for the most common causes of dementia.

3.4 Identify prevalence rates for different types of dementia.

🔑 Key terms

Prevalence: the number of cases

Risk: the likelihood or chance of something happening

Case study

Tom, aged 65 years old, lives on his own and is due to retire from his job as a postman soon. Tom has an active social life and hates the thought of getting old. He plays darts every weekend with his mates, drinks heavily and does not exercise. As a result, Tom is overweight and has hypertension but he rarely visits his GP. Tom's mother lived until she was 80 years old, but died of a dementia-related disease. Tom is worried that he might get dementia too, but is not doing anything to address the possibility. He has decided to take each day as it comes.

1. What factors increase Tom's risk of developing a dementia-related disease?

2. What advice or guidance would you give to Tom about his lifestyle?

3. Whom should Tom contact regarding his weight and hypertension?

Prevalence rates

The **prevalence** rate for dementia is the frequency with which the condition occurs in a population. It has been estimated that by 2021 there will be about 940,000 people living with dementia in the UK. This is expected to rise to 1.7 million by 2051.

The relative frequencies of different forms of dementia are as follows:

- Alzheimer's disease (AD): 62%

- Vascular dementia (VaD): 17%

- Mixed dementia (AD and VaD): 10%

- Lewy body dementia: 4%

- Frontotemporal dementia: 2%

- Parkinson's dementia: 2%

- Other dementias: 3%

Source: Alzheimer's Society (2010)

It is estimated that there are about 15,000 people from black and minority ethnic (BME) communities with dementia in England. This estimate is based on the 2001 census.

The proportion of older people from BME groups in the UK is small but is projected to rise as this section of the population grows older. There is limited published research or statistical information regarding dementia in BME communities.

? Reflect

Why do you think the prevalence rate for dementia is likely to rise over the next few decades? Identify two or three different factors that may explain this trend.

Knowledge Assessment Task

This assessment task covers DEM 201 3.3, 3.4.

The manager of your care setting has asked you to produce an information leaflet for other care professionals and students who visit your workplace to find out about care and services for people living with dementia-related conditions. Many visitors ask about the causes and prevalence of dementia.

You have been asked to produce an information leaflet that:

1. *outlines the risk factors for most common causes of dementia*

2. *identifies the prevalence rates for different types of dementia.*

Your leaflet should provide the information clearly, using words, graphs or other images, and should state the source of any data or statistical information you use.

You should keep a copy of the work that you produce as evidence towards your assessment.

An individual's experience of dementia

Your assessment criteria:

DEM 201

4.1 Describe how different individuals may experience living with dementia, depending on age, type of dementia and level of ability and disability.

4.2 Outline the impact that the attitudes and behaviours of others may have on an individual with dementia.

Living with dementia

This section highlights some of the issues that people living with dementia may face and describes how health and social care practitioners working in statutory and voluntary services can provide them with help and support.

Recognising the symptoms

Living with dementia is not easy. A person with dementia is constantly trying to manage a worsening condition. It may be that in the early stages an individual has decided to keep the condition private, and has not told anyone. It may be that the person does not recognise the signs and symptoms they are experiencing as being the onset of dementia, or has failed to accept the possibility of having developed dementia. In the early stages of dementia, an individual may experience some or all of the following symptoms:

- memory loss

- language difficulty and problems with recalling names and words

- loss of hearing and visual acuity

- changes in behaviour from being a cheerful and responsive person to someone who has become hostile and aggressive with significant mood swings.

? Reflect

Write a brief reflective account of about 100 words of how you would help an individual with a dementia-related condition in your care setting to recognise their symptoms and manage their condition.

Statutory support

In the early stages of dementia an individual experiencing the symptoms described above may be assessed by their local general practitioner (GP) and referred on to a multidisciplinary services team for older people. These teams usually consist of:

- nurses

- speech and language therapists

- occupational therapists

- physiotherapists

- psychologists

- psychiatrists.

Each member of the multidisciplinary team can carry out further assessments of a person's skills, abilities, problems and care needs. These may include a needs-led assessment, which helps determine the individual's strengths and abilities. A member of the team may act as the individual's advocate if the person goes on to lose the ability to make decisions independently or to live safely at home, for example. The outcome of a series of assessments is usually an individualised outreach programme of care, designed specifically to support and empower the person and to maximise their quality of life.

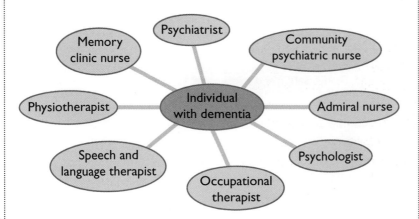

Figure 1.4 The structure of the multidisciplinary team

Investigate

When you are next at your work or placement setting, find out as much as you can from colleagues and members of the multidisciplinary team about the support offered by statutory services for people with dementia-related conditions.

Discuss

Talk to a workplace colleague or classmate about the roles of the multi-disciplinary team in your work setting. Try to identify the various job titles of different care practitioners and how they contribute to dementia care practice.

The role of statutory services is vital for people with dementia-related conditions. Increasingly health and social care practitioners provide support for the families and carers of people affected by dementia. This is important as it helps to maintain the individual's social and support networks and can be the factor that enables them to remain living in their own home.

For those in the early stages of Alzheimer's disease or with undiagnosed memory impairment, a new range of drugs administered by **memory clinic nurses** may be prescribed. These drugs are proving relatively effective: the rate of their success improves the earlier a diagnosis is made. **Admiral nurses** and **community psychiatric nurses** also work with people with dementia (and their families and carers) as outreach workers in the community.

These specialist health and social care practitioners offer a range of support, education and counselling services that can be specially tailored to individuals' needs. Their introduction has also had the effect of increasing the wider community's awareness of dementia, and thus improving the quality of life of those with dementia.

Investigate

Find out where the statutory health care and social services teams for older people with dementia are based in your local area.

Key terms

Admiral nurses: *specialists providing care for people with all forms of dementia and support for their carers in the community*

Community psychiatric nurses: *mental health nurses who work in the community, often with people who have dementia-related conditions*

Memory clinic nurses: *healthcare practitioners who provide drug and other treatments in specialist clinics for people showing early signs and symptoms of memory impairment, particularly Alzheimer's disease*

Case study

Enid and Martin have been married for 50 years and both enjoyed a happy married life. About ten years ago Enid noticed a change in Martin's behaviour. He was a fairly patient and mild mannered man who gradually became very hostile and aggressive, with rapid changes in his mood. One moment he would be happy and laughing, and the next very tearful. He seemed confused at times, finding it difficult to hold a conversation and not remembering his wife's name or those of his two sons.

Eventually Martin agreed to see his GP. While conducting the assessment, Dr White noticed significant memory loss and language difficulties. He informed Martin that he was going to refer him to the multidisciplinary team for older people for a specialist assessment.

1. Identify the symptoms of dementia that Martin is experiencing.

2. Describe who will perform the assessment and what help and treatment you think statutory services should be able to offer Martin and Enid.

3. How can the community psychiatric nurse support Martin in living at home with his wife in the community?

Voluntary support

The voluntary sector has a key role in supporting people with dementia and their families. The *Alzheimer's Society* (www.alzheimers.org.uk) and *Dementia UK* (www.dementiauk.org) provide a useful range of information about dementia issues through their websites. Both organisations work with and on behalf of people with dementia to raise awareness of the common types of dementia, their causes, symptoms and treatments.

In addition to these national bodies, there are many local community based support groups working with people with dementia, their carers and families throughout the UK. These groups are flexible, resourceful and generally easy to access and use. They provide day-to-day support for individuals with dementia, as well as for the family members of individuals with dementia. Their services typically include the provision of:

- practical help

- advice on benefits, treatment and local services

- support to alleviate carers' and sufferers' feelings of isolation.

Voluntary groups are important because they are able to act as links between individuals with dementia and the statutory services.

Investigate

Are there any voluntary organisations or local groups working on behalf of people with dementia in your local area? Try to identify some and find out what services they offer to individuals and their carers or family members.

Inpatient care

Dementia is a progressive illness. This means that every individual's dementia will get worse over time. This often results in people needing inpatient care in a hospital or specialist care home setting. When a person is admitted for inpatient care, tensions can arise because the individual has been placed in an unfamiliar environment. Consequently the person can present a number of challenges that may require careful handling by the healthcare practitioner. These challenges include the person exhibiting violent, argumentative or unresponsive behaviour. This can upset the other patients or residents within an inpatient setting. The individual exhibiting this behaviour could be experiencing a sense of loss or fear in leaving a known environment for another that is alien to them. An individualised, person-centred approach is needed to put the individual at ease, monitor their concerns and promote a sense of wellbeing and harmony. This will subsequently improve the quality of care they receive.

? Reflect

Reflect on the skills you need in order to manage the tensions that may arise when an individual with a dementia-related condition is admitted to an unfamiliar environment. What would you do to promote a sense of wellbeing and harmony for that individual? Write down these thoughts in your journal.

Case study

Margaret Lawrence is a retired 60 year-old woman who had a successful career as a journalist. She is married with three grown-up children and five grandchildren. Margaret lives in the outer suburbs of the city and until recently was a relaxed and pleasant woman who socialised with friends at work and at home. However, since retirement Margaret has found it difficult to engage with her local community or to pursue any of her former social activities, such as yoga and gardening. She is aware that she has not been herself for some time, but has hidden these feelings from her husband and children. Margaret has become forgetful, begun bursting into tears for no apparent reason, developed volatile mood swings and can suddenly become very angry with others. She forgets the time of day and sometimes fails to recognise where she is. Margaret does not know how to cope with the present situation.

1. What signs, symptoms or changes in behaviour suggest that Margaret may have a dementia-related condition?

2. What type of dementia do you think Margaret has?

3. What support services are available for Margaret and for her husband?

Behaviour of others

In the past, some health and social care practitioners may have felt that nothing could be done for people diagnosed with dementia. Attitudes like this may have had a negative impact on the quality and standard of care that some practitioners provided for people with dementia. As a result some people with dementia have been left vulnerable to neglect and abuse by carers, practitioners and others. Negative attitudes and unscrupulous, uncaring behaviour by carers and care practitioners fails to recognise the capabilities and needs of people with dementia or the safeguarding responsibilities of those who are supposed to provide care. However, there has been a shift in attitude in recent years. Dementia is now recognised as a serious and disabling condition requiring the care practitioner's understanding of the individual's lived experience. The shift has been linked to the development and use of the person-centred approach (see next page). This approach values each individual as a unique person regardless of the way they act or communicate. It asks that practitioners tailor their approaches to the needs of the individual who also happen to be a patient, resident or service user. Tom Kitwood, a pioneer of the person-centred approach, recommends the following for those providing care for people with dementia:

- Encourage individuals to tell their life stories, because this helps carers to understand a person with dementia as a distinct individual rather than just as someone with a long-term condition.

- Use pictures and photographs to communicate with and maintain an individual's dignity, particularly in the less personal surroundings of an inpatient facility.

- Protect dignity and seek to reduce embarrassment when providing personal and intimate care for people with dementia.

- Respect each person's privacy and continually promote a person's sense of self through the way care is provided.

 Discuss

Discuss with colleagues, fellow students and your tutor the knowledge and skills that care practitioners require in order to promote a positive attitude to individuals with dementia-related conditions in the care setting.

 Reflect

Think about how you can protect a person's privacy when providing personal and intimate care in order to reduce their embarrassment. Write down your thoughts in your journal.

Knowledge Assessment Task

This assessment task covers DEM 201 4.1, 4.2.

Identify two people with dementia-related conditions from your workplace environment or placement area to focus this activity on. If the people you have chosen are able to communicate verbally, ask each of them to tell you their life story. Alternatively, you could talk to the person's carers, relatives or members of staff in your workplace who know them well. You could also review each person's records for background information. Focus your research, questions and the conversation on:

1. *how the person experiences living with dementia*

2. *what impact the person's dementia has had on their daily living skills*

3. *how the attitudes and behaviours of others have affected the person since they developed the condition.*

Using the information you obtain, create two profiles that:

1. *describe how each person experiences living with dementia*

2. *outline the impact that the attitudes and behaviours of others have had on the individual with dementia.*

Keep the work you produce for this activity as evidence for your assessment.

Person-centred dementia care

Using a person-centred approach

The person-centred approach enables care to be delivered to an individual with dementia in ways that respect the person's values, needs and preferences and which offers them real choice. The emphasis is on including the individual in decision making and helping that person to retain control over their life. It is considered to be the key to good practice and should be an integral part of the delivery of care.

Growth-promoting climate

In terms of developing a successful person-centred approach to care, a working knowledge of the 'growth promoting climate' developed by the American psychologist Carl Rogers is essential. For a growth promoting climate to flourish within the relationship between the individual and the health and social care worker, both parties need to show respect for each other. Individuals with dementia need to feel valued and accepted and must be given the opportunity to achieve their full potential within this relationship. The conditions that should be present for this type of growth to take place include:

- empathy

- unconditional positive regard

- congruence.

Your assessment criteria:

DEM 202

1.1 Describe what is meant by a person-centred approach (see also DEM 204 1.1).

1.2 Outline the benefits of working with an individual with dementia in a person-centred manner.

DEM 204

1.2 Describe how a person-centred approach enables individuals with dementia to be involved in their own care and support.

Key terms

Congruence: arriving at a common agreement

Empathy: conveying to the individual that you understand how they are feeling

Person-centred approach: a package of care negotiated with and delivered to the individual requiring support; it takes account of the needs and wishes of that individual

Unconditional positive regard: means accepting the individual without prejudice

Empathy refers to the ability to appreciate someone else's feelings as if they are your own. This ability can be difficult to learn, because a health or social care worker may not necessarily be experiencing similar feelings to the individual. In practice, experienced dementia care workers summarise what has been said by an individual and the behaviour they observe and relay this back to the person. This is a way of indicating that they have understood the person's feelings.

In order to demonstrate the skill of unconditional positive regard for the individual you need to show genuine concern, honesty, acceptance and warmth when responding to them. If this does not happen, the individual may feel unwanted or unwelcome within that environment. Developing congruence in a therapeutic relationship is much more difficult to achieve, but the care practitioner needs to recognise when agreement is reached between the two parties.

Hierarchy of needs

The person-centred approach takes account of the individual's needs. These needs range from physiological needs, like the needs for shelter, food and air, to high functioning self-rationalised (or actualised) needs, like the needs for non-judgmental conditions, creative outlets and spontaneous activity. With regard to Abraham Maslow's 'hierarchy of needs', each level of needs is dependent on the previous level being adequately catered for. Maslow's hierarchy is presented in the shape of a pyramid and the needs are ranked in the order of importance for human survival. The five descriptions of needs are presented below.

Physiological needs

Physiological needs are represented in the first level and are considered to be the most important set of basic needs that must be satisfied for survival. Every effort should be made to ensure that these basic needs are met for every individual, including those with dementia.

Safety needs

The next level consists of safety and security needs. When all physiological needs are satisfied, the need to feel safe and secure can become a significant issue for the individual. Vulnerable people like those with dementia may display signs of feeling insecure within their environment, as the person can become easily upset, confused or even frightened. The health or social care worker needs to be aware of how the individual is feeling, should try to allay some of those fears and anxieties, and remove any threats from the person's environment that could cause them harm.

 Investigate

Using the internet, your local library and other resources, find out about Carl Rogers' theory of growth promoting climate.

Social needs

Love, affection and belonging are considered to be the social needs that every individual strives for when their physiological and safety needs are satisfied. A person must satisfy their social needs to feel that they belong to a group. If these needs remain unsatisfied, the person can feel isolated and lonely. A person with dementia may find that their social needs are not being met because of the communication difficulties they experience. However, this level should not be ignored. Engagement with health and social care workers and assurance from loved ones are important ways of meeting social needs. Simple things like everyday conversation can help the individual to develop a sense of belonging rather than feeling marginalised. Every individual needs to feel part of a community even if they are residing in a care home.

Self-esteem needs

When the first three levels of needs are satisfied, the individual needs to develop both self-esteem and respect from others. If these needs are not met, the person can feel helpless, weak and worthless. The individual with dementia is worthy of respect regardless of the disability that is being experienced.

Self-actualisation

The final level of Maslow's hierarchy is self-actualisation of needs. This level captures the needs of the individual who uses their talents and abilities to develop their full potential in life. Although this may be perceived as a difficult level of needs to be achieved for the individual with dementia, the whole rationale of person-centred care is to encourage personal growth and fulfilment for those with dementia. Fulfilment may mean different things to different individuals irrespective of disability, so having dementia should not prevent the individual from achieving their true potential.

Figure 1.5 Maslow's hierarchy of needs

 Reflect

How can Maslow's hierarchy of needs be applied to individuals with dementia within your care setting? Can you think of a way in which you help people to meet each type of need in Maslow's hierarchy?

 Investigate

Find out how Maslow's hierarchy of needs is used in the assessment process in the care setting. What kind of information is collected about each of the areas of need that Maslow refers to? You may need to ask your manager or a senior colleague to explain how different areas of need are assessed in your work setting.

Promoting wellbeing

Wellbeing is a term that is frequently used in health and social care settings, and it can mean many different things. When people are asked to define the term, their responses cover ideas ranging from practical matters such as health and financial issues to feelings and emotions such as happiness, contentment, current mental state and hopes for the future. The key characteristics of wellbeing are that a person:

- has a sense of achievement and purpose

- can focus on the positive things in life instead of what can go wrong

- has an active role in society

- is part of a strong, supportive family and community

- feels connected to others and in control of their life

- has financial, emotional and personal security

- lives in a healthy and attractive environment

- has access to appropriate healthcare provision.

In promoting wellbeing and person-centred care with the individual with dementia, health and social care workers need to help the individual to maintain family relationships, friendships and links with their local community. It is important to find out what the person's interests are and to assist them in engaging with them. This will give the individual a sense of purpose in their daily life.

The benefits of working in a person-centred manner

There are several benefits to working with an individual with dementia in a person-centred manner. These are:

- In attempting to provide for all their needs including the promotion of their physical health, it can offer the individual the opportunity to lead as full a life as possible.

- It puts the individual with dementia at the centre of the care planning process and encourages them to be fully involved in the entire process.

- It encourages the health or social care worker to think about the person as an individual and not just someone who has dementia, and to adapt the care given accordingly.

? Reflect

Taking into consideration the key characteristics of wellbeing, consider how you as a health or social care worker would promote an individual with dementia's wellbeing. Think about factors that could affect that person's wellbeing within the practice setting.

- It maintains the individual's **self-identity** and self respect. This is achieved through the concept of **personhood**, the principle upon which person-centred care succeeds or fails.

- It respects the individual's **dignity** and rights which are at the heart of high-quality health and social care.

- It recognises that people from ethnically diverse communities with specific cultural needs would like to be given the opportunity to be more involved in their healthcare.

- It empowers the individual to have choice and some control over the decisions that they are able to make.

- It encourages health and social care workers to provide activities which promote alertness and are responsive to the needs of the individual.

- It acknowledges that the individual has emotions and feelings, and expects the health or social care worker to respond in a warm, affectionate and appropriate manner.

- It recognises the individual's strengths and builds on those leading to a more fulfilling life, rather than focusing on the negative aspects of the long-term condition.

- It enables the individual with dementia to seek the support of advocacy services to make choices about their care or to express their views. Advocates (see page 18) support the individual with making decisions and represent their views when the person is unable to do so.

Person centred care will only succeed if the health or social care workers who are providing an individual with care and support are actually supportive of the approach and also encourage relatives to be central to the caring process.

Investigate

Find out how the benefits of working with an individual in a person-centred manner are embedded in your work place practices, policies and procedures. Do you recognise elements of this approach in your own or other people's care practice?

Key terms

Dignity: *an individual's right to personal privacy and respectful treatment by others*

Personhood: *giving value and respect to the individual with dementia as a person*

Self-identity: *having an understanding of, and being comfortable with one's self*

Knowledge Assessment Task

This assessment task covers DEM 202 1.1, 1.2 and DEM 204 1.1, 1.2.

As a health or social care worker at Fairlawn Nursing Home, you have been asked by your manager to prepare an information sheet for staff in the home on the person-centred approach to care. You are asked to:

1. *describe the meaning of person-centred care*

2. *outline the benefits of using this approach to dementia care practice.*

3. *describe how the person-centred approach is an effective way of enabling individuals to become involved in their own care.*

Keep the written work that you produce for this activity as evidence towards your assessment.

Involving individuals with dementia in their care and support

Personal information

Obtaining personal and life history information from an individual with dementia is an important skill. It provides background and gathers information on particular characteristics and in doing so helps individualise the person. Personal information provides the basis for a person-centred care package.

Life history interview

A person-centred care package begins with a **life history interview**. This interview is intended to:

- obtain personal information

- promote mental stimulation

- prompt recall of past experiences.

The health and social care worker may have to ask other family members, the individual's partner or carers to respond to some of the questions during the life history interview. The interview could be conducted over a period of several weeks in order to present a whole picture of the person's life.

Your assessment criteria:

DEM 204

2.1 Explain how information about personality and life history can be used to support an individual to live well with dementia.

2.2 Communicate with an individual with dementia using a range of methods that meet individual's abilities and needs.

2.3 Involve an individual with dementia in identifying and managing risk for their care and support plan.

2.4 Involve an individual with dementia in opportunities that meet their agreed abilities, needs and preferences.

 Key term

Life history interview: the process by which a health and social care worker learns about the past and the personality of the individual in care

In order to promote mental stimulation, family pictures, war time mementos, music or other items of memorabilia might be used to stimulate memories of past and recent events. Personal information collected may relate to:

- lifestyle – personal habits such as preferences for tea, coffee, alcohol and whether the person smoked, for example

- diet – description of the person's diet, any special diets, and their food preferences

- sleep patterns – description of any difficulties, times of going to bed and getting up, any medication taken

- personal care – personal hygiene, dressing, any difficulties in eating and drinking, elimination patterns

- daily living – relating to home environment, shopping, cooking meals, mobility, managing housework and finances.

The health and social care worker will learn about the individual's childhood, family life, school and job history, beliefs and values and should be able to build a mental picture of the individual as a person with a history.

Using reminiscence therapy

Mental stimulation can be promoted through the use of reminiscence therapy. This therapy helps the individual to recall past experiences and to keep old memories alive. Pictures, songs, newspapers and movies from the person's earlier life can stimulate these memories and can help the individual to remember past events.

Typically an individual with dementia has difficulty in remembering events that occurred recently, but they may also experience lucid moments when recent events can be remembered for a short time span. Try to capture those moments when collecting information.

The information collected for past events could focus on:

- childhood history – early childhood memories of growing up, adolescence, leaving home

- family relationships and family life – parents, siblings, friends and other family members, marriage and children

- education history – level of education attained, schools attended, any difficulties with learning

Key term

Elimination patterns: this term describes the regulation, control and removal of byproducts and wastes in the body

? | Reflect

What kinds of objects, music or foods would stimulate your memories of childhood or early adolescence? Think about things that bring back happy memories of growing up and family relationships.

- job history – past employment, type of jobs and when the person retired

- hobbies/interests – particular hobbies the person likes, membership of any clubs, holidays

- **personality** – specific characteristics of the person, for example whether they are an introvert or an extrovert.

How to carry out a life history interview

The interview process is crucial to the person-centred approach to care and should be conducted regularly as a means of discovering what the individual's needs and wishes are.

The interviews, which should be informal, intimate and conversational, are central to developing and maintaining the carer–client relationship.

When conducting an interview:

- sit close to the person and at the same level, as this suggests that you are on an equal footing

- speak to the person in a calm and reassuring voice

- keep the environment as calm and stress-free as possible

- try to maintain a familiar atmosphere

- keep to a routine that the person is used to

- be consistent in your approach

- encourage the individual to share experiences by nodding appropriately and making eye contact

- lean forward to show interest.

This conversation allows the health or social care worker to build a picture of the individual that goes beyond their present circumstances and is an opportunity to begin to truly empathise with the individual.

In this way, the health or social care worker is able to understand the individual as someone with a knowable personality.

Investigate

Talk with fellow students and your tutor about the kinds of things that might be discussed in a life history interview. If possible, interview a fellow student and share your findings about that person's personality and past with the rest of the group.

Key term

Personality: *specific characteristics and behaviour that are unique to that individual*

Communicating using methods that meet the individual's abilities and needs

Identifying appropriate communication methods

The National Care Forum (2007) suggests that, when using the person-centred approach: 'effective **communication** improves the quality of life of people with dementia. It is essential that efforts are made to enhance communication, make time to listen and understand.' It is important to recognise also that individuals with dementia may only be able to communicative nonverbally through their behaviour rather than through spoken language. As a health or social care worker you need to be able to identify and use methods or forms of communication that are appropriate to each particular individual's needs.

Using different forms of communication

Communication can be verbal or nonverbal. When communicating verbally:

- Use short sentences.

- Avoid direct questions – for example, 'why' questions are direct as they demand an explanation.

- Use open questions – sentences that begin with 'how', 'when', 'who' and 'where'; all provide room for thought, and elicit more information.

- Use closed questions to get factual information – questions that require 'no', 'yes' or single word answers.

- Do not contradict the individual.

- Use active listening skills.

Listening skills are the most important skills that are utilised when engaging in any relationship. Listening is an active process that requires you to be attentive and to concentrate solely on what is being said by the individual. On occasions you may find that you are distracted by noises in the room or by your own private thoughts. This can result in loss of concentration. Once you become aware that this is happening, refocus and continue listening to what is being communicated.

You can assess whether the person is listening to what you are saying by looking at facial expressions and other non-verbal responses if the person's verbal communication is limited. Ask yourself:

Your assessment criteria:

DEM 204

2.2 Communicate with an individual with dementia using a range of methods that meet individual's abilities and needs.

2.3 Involve an individual with dementia in identifying and managing risk for their care and support plan.

2.4 Involve an individual with dementia in opportunities that meet their agreed abilities, needs and preferences.

Key term

Communication: a two-way process by which individuals gain understanding of each other's needs and wishes; it can be verbal or nonverbal

- Is the individual smiling or looking sad?

- Is the person looking bored or angry?

- Is the person paying attention or fidgeting?

- How is the person sitting in the chair?

These are all vital clues that will assist the health and social care worker in developing nonverbal communication skills and responding appropriately to the individual. As a health or social care worker you need to be prepared for the occasions when an individual with dementia may communicate via their behaviour. For example, you may notice aggressive outbursts or crying episodes that seem to occur for no apparent reason. A calm, reassuring approach is required to manage this type of situation. You can minimise barriers to communication by not:

- making assumptions about the person, their abilities or the meaning of their behaviour

- appearing to be cold or indifferent towards them

- looking surprised by the content of the conversation

- being influenced by preconceived ideas regarding the individual.

The person-centred approach can also involve the use of activities and tools to stimulate communication. These could include, for example:

- visual aids – objects that prove successful in stimulating the memory such as, for example, a photo album, a box of mementos that reflect important events in the person's life, a diary, letters, or any other image that represents some aspect of the person's life

- technology – including moving images and sound recordings (speech and music in particular)

- games that stimulate mental activity; for example, playing cards.

Identifying and managing risks

It is important to recognise that individuals with dementia require safeguarding against risk, but also that careless application of safeguarding procedures may unnecessarily affect the rights of the individual, and so negatively impact on the quality of that individual's life. In order to enable individuals with dementia to maintain control over their lives, those caring for them have to balance the benefits of taking risks against the possibility of risk resulting in accident or abuse. A carefully planned person-centred care package must take account of the individual's wishes, and it must accept that some of those wishes may include taking risks.

 Discuss

Spend a few minutes with a colleague asking open and closed questions to familiarise yourself with the type of questions that are used in conversation.

? **Reflect**

Identify an individual with a dementia-related condition and reflect on how you communicate verbally and nonverbally with them. Are you using a person-centred approach as part of your practice?

At the centre of this is the agreement between the individual, significant carers and the organisation as to what constitutes acceptable and unacceptable risk.

Managing risk in practice

1. A number of things can be put in place to make risk acceptable:

2. The care programme is a rolling programme: care is reassessed regularly and responds to any significant change in the individual's circumstances. In this way, risk is gauged against the individual's abilities and capacity to act. The decisions resulting in changes to a programme should always include the individual or the individual's advocate.

3. An audit is conducted regularly as a means of monitoring risks. Risks are recorded and feedback is obtained with regard to the support and care that is received. In any monitoring system, consideration should be given to:

   • when it is appropriate to meet with the individual

   • whether that individual's present state of mood is suited to the task of decision making

   • whether any medicine that has been administered has had the desired effect on that individual. Maintaining the individual's active involvement in the audit places them at the centre of decision making about risk.

4. The environment also needs to be assessed for risks. An environment deemed unacceptable with regard to the level of risk can be alleviated by assistive technologies such as panic buttons and wheelchairs.

However, while the inclusion of these steps minimises risk for the individual, they may initially be perceived by that individual as curtailing personal freedoms. The idea of being wheelchair-bound, for example, may be perceived as restrictive by an individual still able to move without assistance. In this case, the relationship of trust between carer and client is crucial to the task of negotiating a person-centred package that includes acceptable risk. Other factors within the environment should be audited, such as noise levels and the temperature of the rooms. Assess the comfort needs of the individual within the environment, particularly if they are unable easily to convey their feelings to you.

Engaging individuals in their own care

Health and social care workers, and their employing organisation, are responsible for providing individuals with a range of opportunities to meet their particular abilities, needs and preferences. It is important

Key terms

Assistive technologies: devices used to manage risks

Audit: a systematic review of care practices that leads to improvement in care

Reflect

How do you and your colleagues manage the risks to individuals that occur in everyday activities? Is there a set of risk assessment policies and procedures that you refer to? Are there individual risk assessments in individuals' records that you can check?

to get to know each person as an individual and to listen and respond, with due care, to each person's wishes. Involving an individual's partner, family and others involved in their care in this process is important and should be encouraged where these people are able and willing to participate. Strategies for developing opportunities that meet an individual's abilities include:

- conducting a life history interview to obtain a picture of the person, especially their likes and dislikes, skills, abilities and interests

- discussing the individual's abilities and needs with colleagues from other care disciplines, as well as with the individual and/or their advocate where appropriate

- agreeing with the individual a range of activities and opportunities that enable them to use their skills and abilities – including choosing activities, deciding on preferred routines and drawing up a flexible timetable.

All of these strategies should involve the individual concerned so that they 'own' the package of care provided. As a result the person should feel more **empowered**, have their self-esteem boosted and have their sense of identity affirmed.

Reflect

What strategies would you use to involve an individual's partner, family and others in meeting their needs? Think about how you engage individuals in their care as part of your practice.

Key term

Empowered: *enabled to make and carry out decisions affecting your own life*

Practical Assessment Task

This assessment task covers DEM 204 2.1, 2.2, 2.3, 2.4.

This practical assessment task requires you to show that you are able to involve an individual with dementia in the planning and implementation of their care and support using a person-centred approach. With the permission of an individual with dementia (or the permission of their next of kin, where appropriate) and your supervisor or manager, participate in the planning and implementation of person-centred care for the individual. As part of this activity you will need to produce evidence to show that you can:

1. *explain how information about personality and life history can be used to support an individual to live well with dementia*

2. *communicate with the person with dementia using a range of methods that meet the individual's abilities and needs*

3. *involve the person with dementia in identifying and managing risks for their care and support plan*

4. *involve the person with dementia in opportunities that meet their agreed abilities, needs and preferences.*

Your evidence for this task must be based on your practice in a real work environment and must be witnessed by, or be in a format acceptable to, your assessor.

Investigate

Find the members of the multidisciplinary team in your work area. Spend a few minutes talking to them about their roles. Ask them to comment specifically on the person-centred approach to care.

The role of carers in the care and support of individuals with dementia

The importance of carers

Individuals who provide care for their family members or friends are essential components of the person-centred approach to care. They have an important and vital role to play in providing informal care with the support and guidance of professional health and social care workers.

Carers have often acquired a range of practical care skills and a deep understanding of the care needs of their relative. This expertise should be recognised and appreciated by professional health and social care workers.

Health and social care staff should support and encourage carers to share their knowledge and skills and value their contribution in trying to meet the needs of the individual.

Involving and supporting carers

Carers should, wherever possible, be involved in the planning and delivery of their relative's care. This includes involving them in decision making and in working in partnership with the professional care staff. Whatever the reason for an individual's admission to a dementia care setting, a carer may experience feelings of exhaustion coupled with relief and guilt and so will require support.

A referral to a carer's support group may be an option in some cases. A carer's support group will often provide a relative with their first opportunity to express their concerns and frustration, to obtain answers to questions they have and to be given relevant information that can help them in their caring role.

Relationships with carers

Health and social care workers are professional carers who are usually employed in either a residential setting or in a community based dementia care service. They need to develop a **professional** relationship with carers that focuses on the needs of the individual with dementia.

The caring relationship between a health or social care worker and an informal carer is not a friendship based on shared, common interests. Instead it is a work focused relationship that has certain rules and expectations.

This relationship should be focused on the needs of the individual, and therefore both parties need to understand these and have a clear awareness of what person-centred care involves.

Your assessment criteria:

DEM 202

2.1 Describe the role that carers can have in the care and support of individuals with dementia.

2.2 Explain the value of developing a professional working relationship with carers.

DEM 204

3.1 Explain how to increase a carer's understanding of dementia and a person-centred approach.

3.2 Demonstrate how to involve carers and others in the support of an individual with dementia.

🔑 Key terms

Confidentiality: the non disclosure of certain information unless to another authorised person

Professional: maintaining agreed work-related standards

Maintaining confidentiality

Confidentiality can be a significant issue in caring relationships. Health and social care workers need to understand what information about an individual they are able to disclose and share with a partner or other relative and what must remain confidential.

? Reflect

Write a reflective account of how you and the care team involve carers in the person-centred approach within your practice setting.

Knowledge Assessment Task

This assessment task covers DEM 202 2.1, 2.2.

This assessment task requires you to produce a presentation and accompanying handouts to prepare new employees at the Fairlawn Nursing Home for their work.

Your presentation should describe what you see as the role of carers (family, partners, friends and neighbours) in providing care and support for individuals who have dementia. Your handout should explain to new employees the value of developing a professional caring relationship.

Keep a copy of the work that you produce for this activity as evidence towards your assessment.

Practical Assessment Task

This assessment task covers DEM 204 3.1, 3.2.

This practical assessment task requires you to show that you are able to involve carers and others in the care and support of individuals with dementia. The evidence that you produce for this task should be based on your workplace practice.

You should:

1. *write a brief reflective account explaining how you have increased a carer's understanding of dementia and the person-centred approach through your practice*

2. *demonstrate through your practice how to involve carers and others in the support of an individual with dementia.*

Your evidence for this task must be based on your practice in a real work environment and must be witnessed by, or be in a format acceptable to, you and your assessor.

Understanding the role of other professionals

The role of others

There are many other health and social care practitioners who have a key role to play in caring and supporting individuals with dementia. You have already addressed some of these roles in Unit 1 but the list below is far more detailed.

The practitioners are:

- care workers and colleagues who provide physical and social care for those with dementia

- managers who need to provide an inclusive environment in which they respond to the needs of the staff, patients and carers in the healthcare setting and who are committed to providing person-centred dementia care

- social workers who support vulnerable groups of all ages including the older person with dementia

- occupational therapists who assess the individual's daily living activities within their home environment and provide support for the person and carers

- GPs who are normally the first point of contact for individuals with memory problems and who may suspect that the person has dementia

- speech and language therapists who work with individuals who have speech, language and communication problems

- physiotherapists who assist patients with dementia who have mobility problems that may occur either as a result of fractures from falls or from the deterioration of their long-term condition

- pharmacists who aim to provide safe and effective use of medication to the individual with dementia

- nurses who assess and monitor the individual's condition and ensure that the person is receiving the appropriate package of care to meet their specific needs

- psychologists who assess for cognitive decline in the individual who has dementia

- community psychiatric nurses who work in the community, monitor the mental state of the individual who has dementia and provide support for the individual and their carers

Your assessment criteria:

DEM 202

3.1 Describe the role of others in the care and support of individuals with dementia.

3.2 Explain when it may be necessary to refer to others when supporting individuals with dementia.

3.3 Explain how to access the additional support of others when supporting individuals with dementia.

- admiral nurses who are specialists providing care for people with all forms of dementia and support for their carers in the community

- dementia care advisers who support the individual with dementia and their carer and assist them in locating the appropriate services within a specific geographical area.

Benefits of the multidisciplinary team and inter-agency working

Many of the types of practitioner listed above will sit on the multidisciplinary groups that decide on the shape and delivery of the package of care, and all will have a part to play in the care of the individual concerned. You have already looked at the roles of the community psychiatric nurse and admiral nurse (see page 28). However, the list above captures the full multidisciplinary team that is likely to be working with an individual with dementia.

The main goal of the multidisciplinary group is to communicate information to each other regarding the individual so that a comprehensive picture of the individual's needs is produced. A package of care is then devised to meet those needs. The benefits of the team include:

- skills mix

- sharing responsibilities

- support of the team

- need for co-operation

- sharing of information but ensuring confidentiality.

Statutory–voluntary partnerships

In order to work in partnership both the statutory and voluntary organisations need to have shared principles and recognise and accept that both organisations are equally important in improving the quality of care for the individual with dementia. They need to listen to each other and value the work each one is doing.

Advocates are extremely useful when it comes to communicating with individuals during the later stages of dementia. They have particular skills and abilities such as active listening, negotiation and knowledge of legislation.

Discuss

Share your own experiences of working with different members of the multidisciplinary team in a dementia care setting with a work or class colleague. Identify what other team members did and what your role was in relation to theirs.

An Independent Mental Capacity Advocate is normally consulted when either treatment is proposed and there is no relative or known carer who can respond on the person's behalf, or there is a proposal to put an individual in a hospital or care home.

These advocates represent and support the individual, ascertain their wishes and feelings and consider certain courses of action depending on the situation.

Referring to others when supporting individuals with dementia

It is important as a care practitioner to recognise when to refer an individual with dementia, when the service that individual accesses – be it voluntary or statutory – can no longer provide the care and support that the person or their carer requires.

Recognition of the carer's needs is crucial in this context as they can often ignore their own needs and forget about the difficulties they may be experiencing such as lack of sleep, coping with stressful problems, not having enough time for their own interests, struggling with balancing their work and caring role, feeling trapped and generally exhausted.

When the carer can longer manage the individual with dementia within their own home and requires further support, the care practitioner needs to signpost them to the local authorities that may provide them with that much needed help.

The person with dementia and their carer are entitled to separate assessments of their needs. If this assessment highlights that the individual is eligible for services then the local authority has to provide them. Assessment of need has been covered on pages 27–8.

Accessing the support of statutory and voluntary services

Knowing which services individuals with dementia and their carers need to access, whom to ask for advice and which practitioners to put them in touch with are vital information that should be shared with them.

Carers need to be signposted to attend local support groups that encourage them to talk to other individuals who may have had similar experiences and who really understand what it is like to be a carer. The Alzheimer's Society is a good contact for details of local support groups, and local social services departments, the Citizens Advice Bureau, and Carers UK are other useful contacts.

Carers UK runs a number of online discussion forums that can be a useful form of out-of-hours support that can offer practical suggestions on how to cope with a particularly difficult day.

Knowledge Assessment Task

This assessment task covers DEM 202 3.1, 3.2, 3.3.

This assessment task requires you to show that you are able to involve carers and others in the care and support of individuals with dementia. The evidence that you produce for this task should be based on your workplace.

Sheila is a resident at the Fairlawn Nursing Home where you are a care practitioner. Sheila came into the home when her husband had a stroke and could no longer care for her.

Produce a short report to:

1. *describe the role of three professionals who may be involved in providing Sheila's support and care, giving reasons for your choices*

2. *explain two reasons why it may become necessary to refer Sheila for additional support*

3. *explain how you would access this support.*

Your evidence for this task must be in a format acceptable to you and your assessor.

Assessment checklist

The assessment of this unit is partly knowledge-based (assessing things you need to know about) and partly competence-based (assessing things you need to do in the real work environment). To complete this unit successfully, you will need to produce evidence of both your knowledge and your competence.

The knowledge-based assessment criteria for DEM 201, DEM 202 and DEM 204 are listed in the 'What you need to know' table below. The practical or competence-based criteria for DEM 204 are listed in the 'What you need to do' table opposite. Your tutor or assessor will help you to prepare for your assessment, and the tasks suggested in the chapter will help you to create the evidence you need.

Assessment criteria	What you need to know	Assessment task
DEM 201		
1.1	Explain what is meant by the term 'dementia'	Page 15
1.2	Describe the key functions of the brain that are affected by dementia	Page 15
1.3	Explain why depression, delirium and age-related memory impairment may be mistaken for dementia	Page 15
2.1	Outline the medical model of dementia	Page 19
2.2	Outline the social model of dementia	Page 19
2.3	Explain why dementia should be viewed as a disability	Page 19
3.1	List the most common causes of dementia	Page 23
3.2	Describe the likely signs and symptoms of the most common causes of dementia	Page 23
3.3	Outline the risk factors for the most common causes of dementia	Page 25
3.4	Identify prevalence rates for different types of dementia	Page 25
4.1	Describe how different individuals may experience living with dementia depending on age, type of dementia and level of ability and disability	Page 31
4.2	Outline the impact that the attitudes and behaviours of others may have on an **individual with** dementia	Page 31

Assessment criteria	What you need to know	Assessment task
DEM 202		
1.1	Describe what is meant by a person-centred approach	Page 36
1.2	Outline the benefits of working with an individual with dementia in a person-centred manner	Page 36
2.1	Describe the role that carers can have in the care and support of individuals with dementia	Page 45
2.2	Explain the value of developing a professional working relationship with carers	Page 45
3.1	Describe the roles of others in the care and support of individuals with dementia	Page 49
3.2	Explain when it may be necessary to refer to others when supporting individuals with dementia	Page 49
3.3	Explain how to access the additional support of others when supporting individuals with dementia	Page 49
DEM 204		
1.1	Describe what is meant by a person-centred approach	Page 36
1.2	Describe how a person-centred approach enables individuals with dementia to be involved in their own care and support	Page 36

Assessment criteria	What you need to do	Assessment task
DEM 204		
2.1	Explain how information about personality and life history can be used to support an individual to live well with dementia	Page 43
2.2	Communicate with an individual with dementia using a range of methods that meet individual's abilities and needs	Page 43
2.3	Involve an individual with dementia in identifying and managing risks for their care and support plan	Page 43
2.4	Involve an individual with dementia in opportunities that meet their agreed abilities, needs and preferences	Page 43
3.1	Explain how to increase a carer's understanding of dementia and a person-centred approach	Page 45
3.2	Demonstrate how to involve carers and others in the support of an individual with dementia	Page 45

2 | Communication and interaction with individuals with dementia

DEM 205
LO1 Understand the factors that can influence communication and interaction with individuals who have dementia

▶ Explain how dementia may influence an individual's ability to communicate and interact

▶ Identify other factors that may influence an individual's ability to communicate and interact

▶ Outline how memory impairment may affect the ability of an individual with dementia to use verbal language

DEM 205
LO2 Understand how a person-centred approach may be used to encourage positive communication with individuals with dementia

▶ Explain how to identify the communication strengths and abilities of an individual with dementia

▶ Describe how to adapt the style of communication to meet the needs, strengths and abilities of an individual with dementia

▶ Describe how information about an individual's preferred methods of communication can be used to reinforce identity and uniqueness

DEM 205
LO3 Understand the factors which can affect interactions with individuals with dementia

▶ Explain how understanding about an individual's biography/history can facilitate positive interactions

▶ List different techniques that can be used to facilitate positive interactions with an individual with dementia

▶ Explain how involving others may enhance interaction with an individual with dementia

CHAPTER 2

DEM 210
LO1 Be able to communicate with individuals with dementia

▶ Describe how memory impairment can affect the ability of an individual with dementia to use verbal language

▶ Gather information from others about an individual's preferred methods of communicating to enhance interaction

▶ Use information about the communication abilities and needs of an individual with dementia to enhance interaction

▶ Use a person-centred approach to enable an individual to use their communication abilities

▶ Demonstrate how interaction is adapted in order to meet the communication needs of an individual with dementia

DEM 210
LO2 Be able to apply interaction and communication approaches with individuals in dementia

▶ List different techniques that can be used to facilitate positive interactions with an individual with dementia

▶ Use an individual's biography/ history to facilitate positive interactions

▶ Demonstrate how the identity and uniqueness of an individual has been reinforced by using their preferred methods of interacting and communicating

Introduction to this chapter

This chapter focuses on the knowledge and skills you need in order to communicate and interact effectively with individuals who have dementia. It describes the ways in which dementia impacts on communication through changes related to verbal language and understanding.

It also explores the concept of a person-centred approach to communication, where communication and interaction styles and techniques are adapted in ways that support and reinforce the unique individuality of each person. The chapter covers everything you need to know to complete two closely related units of the level 2 Dementia Care Award and Certificate: DEM 205 and DEM 210.

Your assessment criteria:

DEM 205

1.1 Explain how dementia may influence an individual's ability to communicate and interact.

1.2 Identify other factors that may influence an individual's ability to communicate and interact.

1.3 Outline how memory impairment may affect the ability of an individual with dementia to use verbal language.

DEM 210

1.1 Describe how memory impairment can affect the ability of an individual with dementia to use verbal language.

The influence of dementia on communication and interaction

The physiological damage of dementia, such as lack of blood circulation to areas of the brain and degeneration of brain cells, affects those areas of the brain that are involved in **communication** and **interaction**. This interferes in a range of ways with a person's ability to exchange information and make meaningful contact with others. Some of these changes are set out in the diagram (figure 2.1) below.

Be aware that not every person with dementia will have their ability to communicate and interact affected in the same way. For example: some individuals might retain their social skills to chat about fairly superficial matters such as the weather, and continue with social conventions such as saying please and thank-you.

Other individuals may not be able to comprehend social conventions and interrupt and ignore those who are speaking, or stop speaking altogether.

Key terms

Agnosia: an inability to recognise what objects are and what they are meant for or who people are

Aphasia: partial or total loss of the ability to speak or write

Communication: the exchange of information between people using speech and non-verbal means

Interaction: the interplay (contact and responses) between people

Lucidity: ability to think clearly

Memory impairment: difficulty in creating or recalling memories of recent or past events

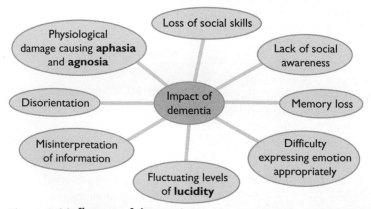

Figure 2.1 Influence of dementia on communication and interaction

The effects of memory impairment on verbal language

Communication is about making contact with one another and being understood and a major way to communicate is through speech and having conversations. Most people are able to do this almost without thinking, but for those with dementia the impact of memory impairment can make verbal language more difficult, both to speak and to understand. Dementia interferes with a person's ability to process information, remember it and express it accurately. Have a look at the table below (figure 2.2), which sets out the main difficulties that arise.

? Reflect

Think over a recent conversation you have had in your work or placement setting with a person with dementia who has memory impairment. How did the person express him or herself and what verbal language impairments did you notice as you communicated?

Figure 2.2 Verbal language difficulties

Verbal language difficulties	Example
Choosing an incorrect word to express feelings	Saying 'tired' when meaning 'sad'
Only being able to find single words to express complex feelings	Saying 'worried' when in fact the person is experiencing a mixture of anxiety, uncertainty, grief and a sense of loss
Talking fluently, but words do not appear to make sense, (sometimes referred to as 'word salad')	Such as, 'the talking microphone is table up and off'
Creating new words where the meaning is not clear	Such as, 'telebockteen'
Choosing words that are similar – in meaning or sound – to the intended word, but are not quite accurate	Such as saying, 'he's got a hairy' when commenting that someone has a beard, or stating, 'he has a bread'
Repeating sounds and words that others say, but without understanding	Like an echoing of what has been last heard
Losing the ability to start or follow a conversation	Therefore unable to grasp the full meaning of what is said
Partially or fully misunderstanding conversation	Not making connections and inaccurately interpreting what is being said
Using challenging or demeaning language, including swearing	'You're very fat/ugly', and so on
Having a shortened concentration span and being unable to focus for long enough to enable understanding	Care practitioners must therefore speak clearly in short sentences, giving concise information, such as, 'I will help you to dress in your clothes' (while pointing to clothes as a visual cue) rather than 'It's morning time so I'll help you get up and about now, ready to meet the new day'
Losing the ability to speak a second language, lapsing into their first language	A person might be able to repeat the information in English if prompted

It can be immensely frustrating and upsetting for a person with dementia to cope with disruption to their verbal language skills. A care practitioner who takes time and shows empathy, both in trying to understand what a person wants to express as well as finding alternative ways of communicating, will make all the difference to how a person experiences their dementia.

Key terms

Delusional ideas: *a fixed belief or perception that persists despite evidence to the contrary*

Empathy: *understanding another person's feelings as if they are your own by imagining things from their perspective*

Paranoia: *an unfounded or exaggerated negative state of distrust towards objects and people which can form part of a delusion*

Case study

Dorothea has started to attend Broadmead day centre for people with dementia. Her daughter tells staff members that her mother has become isolated at home and cut off from activities she previously enjoyed, such as a creative writing group and an art class.

She explains that Dorothea stopped going to these because her memory impairment made it hard for her to join in with conversations and she felt embarrassed when she forgot or misunderstood things and lost track of what was being said.

During their initial look around staff notice that the daughter tends to speak on Dorothea's behalf and in the first week of attendance she remains very quiet, tending to give the same answers to questions, such as, 'if you think so, dear' or, 'whatever you think best'.

One morning when they are painting greetings cards Dorothea bursts into tears, saying over and over, 'so sad, so sad, so sad'.

1. In what different ways has memory impairment impacted on Dorothea's verbal language skills?

2. Why do you think Dorothea's daughter speaks for her and what do you think about this?

3. From what you know of Dorothea, what do you imagine she is trying to express by the repetition of her words, 'so sad'?

Other factors influencing ability to communicate and interact

As well as the influence of dementia on communication and interaction there are other factors that also have an impact. Some of these may happen because a diagnosis of dementia means a person can no longer run their life the way they could before and may need to have support services, or even move out of their own home. They may not even feel like they are the same person any more and this will influence how they communicate and interact.

Have a look at the diagram below (figure 2.3) which provides an overview of other factors that can impact on communication and interaction.

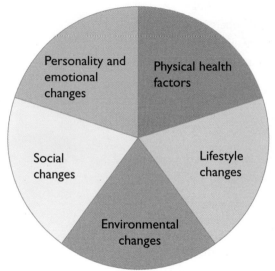

Figure 2.3 The influence of other factors on communication and interaction

- **Personality and emotional factors**: a person can become more emotionally labile, which means having less control over emotions and moving between different emotions – such as sadness, laughter and anger – where triggers are not obvious. There may also be evidence of paranoia and delusional ideas, which can make a person suspicious and less trusting.

- **Physical health factors**: think about medical issues other than dementia, such as the 'mask-like' face of Parkinson's disease that affects facial muscles, making it difficult for a person to show emotion when interacting, or someone with a stroke who finds it difficult to form words. Also if a person is in pain or feeling nauseated it reduces their desire to be sociable. Remember, too, that dementia may interfere with a person being able to report physical symptoms, which means that making observations (such as whether a person is having regular bowel motions and eating well) and recording and passing these on takes on additional importance.

- **Social changes**: in some care environments there may be fewer stimuli and it is possible for a person with dementia to become bored and withdraw into their own world. Or there might be other people who exhibit disturbing behaviours and interfere or become aggressive, making building relationships difficult.

- **Environmental changes**: think about the changes that may have taken place to make adaptations to a person's home, or consider the changes experienced in being admitted to hospital or residential care. This can have a disorientating effect and be frightening and confusing.

- **Lifestyle changes**: think about the impact, for example, of needing to have additional support from family and care workers, where a loss of independence and changes to normal routines are difficult to accept. This may affect relationships and normal communication and interaction.

Knowledge Assessment Task

This assessment task covers DEM 205 1.1, 1.2, 1.3 and DEM 210 1.1.

Health and social care practitioners who work with individuals with dementia need to understand how dementia can influence a person's ability to communicate and interact, including the ways in which memory impairment can affect verbal language, as well as the impact of other associated factors. To carry out this assessment task you need to:

1. *produce a leaflet suitable for relatives of people with dementia to explain the different factors that can influence communication and interaction*

2. *make sure you include the specific ways in which a person's ability to communicate and interact can be affected by:*

   - *dementia*

   - *other factors*

   - *the ways that verbal language can be affected.*

Keep the written work that you produce for this activity as evidence towards your assessment. Your assessor may also want to ask you questions about the way you communicate with individuals with dementia in the work setting.

Reinforcing individual identity through person-centred communication

Communicating with the unique individual

Each person with dementia whom you interact and communicate with is, first and foremost, a unique individual. Your communication and interaction must be all about building a relationship that recognises and reflects their individuality.

Using a person-centred approach

Enabling communication with a person with dementia who experiences communication difficulties requires you to place them at the centre, that is, to use a person-centred approach to communicating and interacting. It is all about building a positive relationship with the person and establishing a good **rapport**.

To achieve this you need to demonstrate each of the aspects set out in the diagram on the next page (figure 2.4) during your interactions. These are further explained below the diagram.

Your assessment criteria:

DEM 205

2.1 Explain how to identify the communication strengths and abilities of an individual with dementia.

2.3 Describe how information about an individual's preferred methods of communication can be used to reinforce identity and uniqueness.

3.1 Explain how understanding about an individual's biography/history can facilitate positive interactions.

DEM 210

1.4 Use a person-centred approach to enable an individual to use their communication abilities.

2.2 Use an individual's biography/history to facilitate positive interactions.

2.3 Demonstrate how the identity and uniqueness of an individual has been reinforced by using their preferred methods of interacting and communicating.

 Key term

Rapport: a connection between two people, where the relationship is based on mutual understanding, emotional warmth and good communication

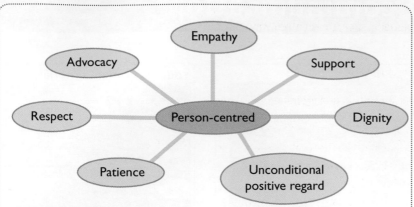

Figure 2.4 Demonstrating a person-centered approach

Key terms

Advocacy: *representing a person's viewpoint, preferences, choices and decisions and looking after the interests of a person who cannot stand up for him or herself*

Life story: *a record of the person's memories and their past life*

Unconditional positive regard: *acting in ways that show you accept and respect an individual for the person they are, without prejudice or discrimination*

- **Respect**: speaking and acting in a manner that conveys that you value and accept a person, including their beliefs and ideas. Also putting them at the centre of a decision-making process, not speaking for them without their agreement, over the top of them, or behind their back and avoiding contradicting them

- **Empathy**: demonstrating sensitivity and an ability to understand things from the other person's viewpoint, without necessarily even needing to express this in words

- **Unconditional positive regard**: behaving in ways that demonstrate your view of a person as being worthy of your attention, no matter who they are, what they believe, where they come from and what they do

- **Dignity**: preserving the person's sense of self, even when this has been diminished by the effects of dementia, such as not laughing if they say something inadvertently rude or unintentionally funny

- **Patience**: allowing enough time for proper communication to take place, showing a calm and unhurried manner, trying not to rush what a person says, or to speak over them

- **Support**: encouraging and enabling communication and interaction abilities to optimise the different ways in which a person can express him or herself

- **Advocacy**: making yourself aware of what is important to the person and representing this to others on their behalf when the person is unable to, and doing so in a way that supports and protects their preferences and choices

Communicating with each unique individual in a person-centred way requires two processes to come together:

- Identifying communication strengths and abilities

- Recognising preferred methods of communication and interaction

When you communicate and interact with a person with dementia you should observe what works well and build on the communication strengths and abilities you notice. For example, a person may have difficulty remembering names and faces, but might still be able to remember the lyrics of songs or poems they learned in school. In such a case, you might find that you succeed with a task that needs to be done, such as helping the person have a bath, if you spend the time singing with them as well. In this way you are acknowledging the unique individual and relating in a way that shows you value the person.

It might become clear that a person prefers to use gestures and touch to express their thoughts and needs and you can mirror this behaviour, which lets them know you are happy to use this form of communication and recognise that this works best for them.

You should be able to recognise the types of communication style and specific communication techniques that will suit interaction with each person, bearing in mind that this might involve a range of different styles and techniques at different times and in different situations. See pages 65–9 for more about this.

A process known as 'enriched care planning' can help to bring all these strands together. This was developed because of a realisation that people with dementia who live in residential care settings can become disengaged with their surroundings and the people around them when care practitioners fail to recognise their individual changing needs. Consequently, they can become more unwell and more seriously affected by dementia. This method assesses the five areas of life-story, personality, health, neurological impairment and social psychology to provide suggestions for tailored interventions for each person based on the profile that emerges from the assessment process.

Using life stories

When dementia is wearing away a person's sense of self, your communication can relate to and remind them of the person they still are inside. This is where it is so important to find out about a person's **life story**, also known as life histories or biographies. Finding out this information is mutually beneficial, sometimes giving you fascinating insights to a social history of times past and helping you and the individual to build a relationship together.

 Reflect

Identify one particular person with dementia with whom you work. Think about how you can demonstrate your respect for him or her, through your words and actions.

 Discuss

Talk together with colleagues about some different ways you can use communication to be an advocate for those individuals with dementia with whom you work.

 Investigate

Using work, library and internet sources, find out information about enriched care planning and life story work with older people with dementia.

The aim of the life story is to build up a picture of a person's life that provides you with an excellent foundation for communication by:

- telling you about the person before they were affected by dementia

- gathering relevant facts that you can use as triggers for conversation

- providing information that you can reflect back to the person to help rebuild their sense of self

- giving you insights into their personality and experiences and helping you to form a closer relationship.

When you create a life story it is a good idea to find out about a range of subject areas. Have a look at the diagram below (figure 2.5) for some suggestions.

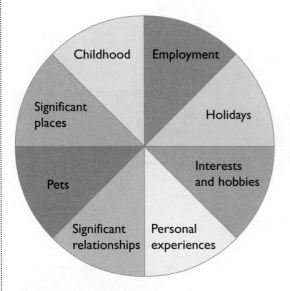

Figure 2.5 Life story topic areas

Find out information for life stories by asking the person questions about their past life experiences, perhaps using memorabilia as a prompt, such as photographs and pictures; also artefacts (for example, an old-fashioned iron, a toy, such as a wooden abacus or a humming-top and pre-decimal money).

Popular music from the time of their youth or World War II might equally stimulate a conversation. Family members and friends can provide memorabilia and help to fill in any gaps – indeed, this can be a pleasurable exercise for all involved to do together.

 Investigate

Using work, library, local council and internet sources, find out about reminiscence resources in your local area. Some museums run schemes for lending memorabilia.

? Reflect

Identify an individual with a dementia-related condition in your work or placement setting. Consider the specific ways you communicate with that person that demonstrate a person-centred approach.

Case study

Mr Fortesque has been in respite care since his wife's recent death. He experiences severe memory impairment due to dementia and has no insight into this.

Mr Fortesque has settled well, believing he is at his golf club and most of the time that he is either about to have a game of golf or has just had one. His sons have brought in his golf bag and he always wears the associated clothing. They explain that their father is a cheerful person with a great sense of humour.

He gets on well with all the care staff, enjoying lots of banter, but especially with the manager whom he mistakes for his wife and refers to as, 'my wife – the boss'. A new care worker is helping Mr Fortesque get dressed, selecting clothes from his wardrobe and laying them out. Mr Fortesque, seeing clothes that seem unfamiliar, suddenly shouts loudly, 'This won't do. Tut tut. Fetch the wife! She's the boss.'

The care worker, alarmed by the volume of his voice, assumes he is angry. She tells him he must not shout and that his wife has died, which is why he is in a care home and why she is helping him dress. Mr Fortesque looks shocked and distressed and charges out of the room in his pyjamas roaring, 'I need the boss' at the top of his voice.

1. Given the information you know about Mr Fortesque, how could the care practitioner have acted in a more person-centred way?

2. What are Mr Fortesque's communication and interaction strengths and abilities, and how could the care practitioner build on these?

3. In what ways might building a life story help the care practitioner and Mr Fortesque provide person-centred care?

Knowledge Assessment Task

This assessment task covers DEM 205 2.1, 2.3, 3.1

Care practitioners need to be able to recognise the communication strengths, abilities and preferences of those people with dementia with whom they work and use this and knowledge of their life story to enable positive interactions and reinforce the person's identity and uniqueness.

To complete this task you need to:

1. *think about your own life and create a life story, focusing on significant events and people, places and milestones, your likes and dislikes and your hobbies and interests*

2. *describe your own reflections on how building your own life story has reinforced your own identity and uniqueness*

3. *drawing on the above exercise, think about a person with dementia whom you work with and create a spider diagram to set out their communication strengths, abilities and preferences*

4. *add a short description for each to link this to the ways these strengths, abilities and preferences relate to their sense of identity.*

Keep the written work that you produce for this activity as evidence towards your assessment. Your assessor may also want to ask you questions about the way you communicate with individuals with dementia in the work setting.

Practical Assessment Task

This assessment task covers DEM 210 1.4, 2.2, 2.3

Identify a person with dementia whom you provide care for. Make sure you are familiar with their preferred ways of communicating and their life story, and that you are aware of the significance these hold for person-centred work. Arrange for your assessor to observe you interacting in a person-centred way with this person in your work setting.

Your practice should demonstrate that you are able to:

1. *use an individual's biography/history to facilitate positive interactions*

2. *use a person-centred approach to enable the individual to use their communication abilities*

3. *demonstrate how the identity and uniqueness of an individual has been reinforced by using their preferred methods of interacting and communicating.*

Your evidence for this task must be based on your practice and experience in a real work environment.

Adapting communication style and applying techniques

Your assessment criteria

DEM 205

2.2 Describe how to adapt the style of communication to meet the needs, strengths and abilities of an individual with dementia.

3.2 List different techniques that can be used to facilitate positive interactions with an individual with dementia.

DEM 210

1.5 Demonstrate how interaction is adapted in order to meet the communication needs of an individual with dementia.

2.1 List different techniques that can be used to facilitate positive interactions with an individual with dementia.

The reasons for adapting communication styles and techniques

Verbal communication can be difficult and frustrating for a person with dementia. Gaps in the memory may have resulted in embarrassing situations for the person, from the inconvenience of forgetting facts like the current date and time, to the traumatic loss of intimate personal knowledge, such as the names of their own children or spouse. It can feel safer to choose not to talk, leading to isolation and social withdrawal. As a care practitioner, it is important to continue encouraging the individual to communicate and interact, by:

• adapting your communication style

• emphasising non-verbal communication

• using communication techniques.

Adapting communication style

It is possible to adapt the usual ways in which you communicate to encourage and enable communication in others. Some of these adaptations you probably do intuitively, but it is a good idea to become more aware, making it a conscious process that you can build on. Some occasions might call for a particular communication style and sometimes a range of communication styles might be required within one interaction with a person. Have a look at the table below (figure 2.6), which describes a number of adaptations you can make to your communication style.

Key term

Body language: *a way of communicating without speech, which includes both conscious elements, such as gestures and signs and automatic responses, such as posture and facial expression*

Figure 2.6 Adapting communication and interaction style

Communication and interaction style	Adaptation
Use humour. Be wary of asking too many questions.	Puts the person at their ease and helps them to feel relaxed. This can put pressure on a person and make them feel they are being tested.
Non-verbal communication, also called body language, includes: gestures, posture, body-orientation, proximity, facial expression, eye-contact and touch.	Body language is a communication method all of its own. It can also be used to emphasise your spoken language and provide clues about the meaning of words spoken by a person with dementia.
Tone of voice – conveys an emotional message behind the spoken words. Pitch of voice – concerns how low or high your voice is.	People with dementia may be sensitive to tone of voice and will, for example, pick up if a person is impatient. Speaking in a low voice can be calming and soothing, but too low and you can sound boring.
Reminiscence is a form of remembering that focuses on a person's past and taps into memories that are still intact, such as of childhood, family and working life. Reminiscence can be comforting and affirm a person's unique individuality.	Use the senses to evoke verbal responses, prompted by: • hearing – such as favourite songs and music from the person's era, for example the 1940s or wartime • sight – through photos, pictures • smell – through evocative scents (vanilla, orange, shoe polish) which relate to memories • taste – through flavours that conjure memories, such as sweets from childhood or certain meals • touch – objects with meaning for the person.
Validation therapy is a way of communicating that focuses on the emotion behind words and supports the person saying it.	Even if what is spoken by a person with dementia does not make sense, or is factually incorrect and does not fit with reality, do not dismiss it as rambling nonsense, but look for the feeling behind the message. The person is letting you know about their reality, which holds meaning for them and is therefore valid.
Reality orientation assists confused or disoriented persons to be aware of the 'here and now', by emphasising the time, day, month, year, situation and weather.	At times this style of communication can help a person to feel more secure and aware of their immediate surroundings.

Emphasising non-verbal communication

Non-verbal communication is a crucial element of your interaction and can enhance the verbal messages you send, as well as telling you more about the communication of others. For example, an open posture and smiling facial expression can help a person relax and by showing concern through your expression you may help a person confide in you. Be aware of communicating body language messages you do not mean to convey, such as rolling your eyes, tutting and sighing while looking at your watch, which clearly indicate that you are bored, or perhaps anxious about time and impatient to hurry away. Have a look at the diagram (figure 2.7) and the explanations that follow.

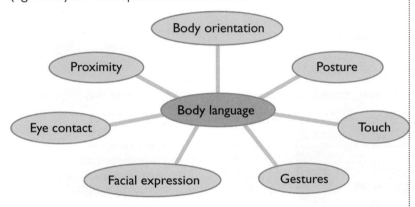

Figure 2.7 The elements of non-verbal communication

- **Proximity:** is about the distance between people. How close we stand or sit to a person relates to intimacy and it can feel intimidating if a person invades body space by getting too close. Many care interventions necessitate getting physically close to a person and touching them, often in intimate areas, so be sensitive to allowing greater body space at other times and not crowding or overwhelming a person.

- **Body orientation:** is about the direction of your body in relation to another person. Be aware of not standing squarely in front of a person, which can feel aggressive and confrontational. However, if your body is turned away from a person it might be interpreted as lack of interest.

- **Posture:** is about the stance of your body and can reveal your attitude. For example, having your arms folded across your front can make you appear guarded or even defensive.

- **Touch:** can be used to provide reassurance and guidance, such as a pat or stroke to arm or shoulder and a gentle squeeze of a person's hand. However, it should be used with sensitivity as some people with dementia do not like to be touched and interpret this as an invasion or even an attack. Touch is also a safeguarding issue when you work with vulnerable people and you must never impose yourself physically on anyone.

 Reflect

Take time to observe the non-verbal behaviour of an older person with whom you work. Also notice the non-verbal behaviour of staff members working with this person. Think about what this might tell you.

 Discuss

Talk together with colleagues about the use of touch to communicate empathy when working with older people with dementia, including discussing the need to be sensitive about ensuring touch is appropriate and welcomed.

Investigate

Using work, library and internet sources, find out information about validation therapy and ways to use this in your working practice with older people with dementia.

- **Gestures**: are signs made with the hands and arms to illustrate or emphasise your words or to stand in place of words. People often gesticulate during conversations without really thinking about it, but you can use gestures deliberately to make your meaning more clear. Be careful because not all gestures are universal and instead of clarifying a message you could create confusion, especially if the person is from a different cultural background.

- **Facial expression**: reveals a great deal about our feelings. Think of a grimace of pain, a wide grin of happiness or a worried frown. In fact, a blank facial expression makes it much harder to interpret what is being said.

- **Eye contact**: is about your gaze, which during most conversations will flit to and from another person's face. Holding someone's gaze is a sign of intimacy, but to do so with a person you don't know well can feel uncomfortable or even threatening.

Using communication techniques

There are a number of specific techniques to help a person with communication difficulties to express themselves – this may be verbally, or through non-verbal communication. Figure 2.8 opposite describes some commonly used techniques.

 Reflect

Take time to think about active listening and whether you practise this on a regular basis each day. Raise your awareness to really listening before you rush in to speak or answer someone.

 Discuss

Share with colleagues the techniques you use to make contact and have meaningful communication with people with whom you work who have dementia and who are unable to speak or hold conversations.

Investigate

Using work, library and internet sources, find out information about communication boards that have been designed for use with older people with dementia.

 Key terms

Communication boards and talking mats: *aids that use visual symbols and different textures to help a person communicate about needs, wishes and preferences*

Makaton: *a form of sign language that uses signs and symbols alongside speech to support verbal communication*

Figure 2.8 Using communication techniques

Communication technique	Method
Provide a conducive environment to enable communication	Make sure the room is quiet, without distraction
	Turn off TV
	Position chairs at an angle, rather than side by side, which is more comfortable and less formal
	If the person is reluctant to talk, use a social situation, such as having a meal together, to create a situation more conducive to conversation
Maximise understanding	Face the person, speaking clearly and calmly
	Maintain positive eye contact without staring
	Simplify your speech to avoid overloading your message with unnecessary words
Active listening	Focus on really tuning in to the person's speech and taking in what is being communicated, including non-verbal information. Make sure you show you are listening through your non-verbal communication
Provide prompts	Pointing to objects or people
	Using reality orientation prompts, such as newspaper, calendar, clock
	Using reminiscence memorabilia
Use alternative languages	Sign language, such as Makaton, which supplements spoken works with specific signs for objects and actions
Use appropriate aids	Writing and drawing messages can sometimes be easier than verbal communication, but dementia can mean that writing and drawing skills decline even before speech does
	Communication boards and talking mats are used by the person to indicate feelings, needs and preferences. Boards are available that have been designed for specific situations, such as going to the doctor

Case study

Birgita is the resident who has lived the longest at Highlands care home – she has been there even longer than every member of the present staff team. Her dementia has progressed to the point where Birgita barely ever speaks. She sits all day in a large armchair, and for much of that time appears to be asleep, but sometimes she looks around the room and does seem to be taking notice.

Ruby is a new manager at the home and is trying to get to know all the residents, but is struggling to find ways to make meaningful contact with Birgita. When Ruby discusses this with Maggie, the activities coordinator, Maggie retorts, 'You can't get through to all of them. I don't think Birgita really likes contact with others – she's probably always been the same way'.

1. What do you think about Maggie's attitude to Birgita?

2. What styles or techniques of communication do you suggest the manager tries?

3. Why do you think each of your suggestions might work?

Knowledge Assessment Task

This assessment task covers DEM 205 2.2, 2.3, 3.2.

Care practitioners need to adapt their communication style and use a variety of communication techniques in order to have positive interactions with individuals with dementia and meet their differing communication needs, strengths and abilities.

To complete this task, you need to imagine that you have been asked to work alongside a new member of staff to help them develop their communication skills. Produce some teaching materials, such as handouts or a PowerPoint presentation about:

1. *different methods of adapting communication style*

2. *a range of communication techniques*

3. *how to identify and build on the communication strengths and abilities of a person with dementia.*

You can use examples of individuals from your working practice to illustrate your teaching materials, but be careful not to use their real names, for confidentiality purposes.

Keep the written work that you produce for this activity as evidence towards your assessment. Your assessor may also want to ask you questions about the way you communicate with individuals with dementia in the work setting.

Practical Assessment Task

This assessment task covers DEM 210 1.5, 2.1.

Your knowledge about the specific communication needs of a person with dementia whom you provide care for will help you to adapt your interactions to meet these and facilitate positive interactions.

To complete this task you need to:

1. *create a document, such as a care plan that identifies the communication needs of an individual with dementia whom you provide care for and sets out the different ways in which you meet these needs*

2. *arrange for your assessor to observe you interacting with this person in your work setting, where your practice demonstrates some ways in which you adapt your communication style and method.*

Your evidence for this task must be based on your practice and experience in a real work environment.

Working together to support communication

People and places for finding out information

You can find information about ways to enhance communication with older people with dementia from a number of sources. It is probable that most individuals with dementia have a network of people involved in giving care and support, either formally as practitioners, or informally as family members, friends and neighbours. Between all these people there will be a wealth of information about the person's communication difficulties and the best ways to manage these and enhance interaction.

Involving others to enhance communication

There is a wide range of people who can help to enhance communication for people with dementia:

- **Family members and friends** have a crucial role to play as they know the person best, have insights into their behaviour and feelings and will be sensitive to their body language. Importantly, they will be able to advise you whether or not the use of physical contact (touch) will help to encourage the individual to communicate, as well as letting you know specific familiar words for items, subject areas that interest them and topics that might cause distress and are best avoided.

- **Health and social care support workers** may have worked with the individual over a long time and with experience have come to understand the best methods to communicate and interact to provide effective care. As well as being aware of aids required for communication, such as spectacles, hearing aids, magnifying glasses and so on, they will recognise familiar patterns of behaviour and preferred routines and be able to offer you useful insights.

- **Other workers within a residential setting** such as cleaners, maintenance staff and the chef, as well as visiting practitioners such as the hairdresser and podiatrist, are likely to have a different sort of relationship with the person. They may be able to offer encouragement or perhaps reassurance and relate in a relaxed manner.

- Social workers arrange, assess, review and oversee care services for those with dementia and their families, both at home and within residential care services. In this way they provide a useful link for communication between the two environments.

Your assessment criteria:

DEM 205

3.3 Explain how involving others may enhance interaction with an individual with dementia.

DEM 210

1.2 Gather information from others about an individual's preferred methods of communicating to enhance interaction.

1.3 Use information about the communication abilities and needs of an individual with dementia to enhance interaction.

 Key term

Social workers: *registered social care practitioners who support vulnerable groups of all ages including older people with dementia*

- Nurses have experience of communicating with individuals with dementia to provide personal and intimate care, as well as necessary health treatments and interventions. They are likely to recognise non-verbal communication that suggests a person is in pain, uncomfortable or anxious.

- Speech and language therapists are trained to diagnose and analyse communication problems in individuals and will be able to suggest strategies and tips and provide aids to improve communication for people with dementia.

- Occupational therapists assess the individual's daily living activities, both within home and care environments, and provide aids to help a person and their carers to manage needs, including communication needs.

- Community psychiatric nurses work in community settings to monitor the mental health of individuals with dementia. They are skilled in interpreting behaviours to recognise what a person is trying to communicate, as well as recognising signs and symptoms of mental illness that may impact on communication, such as hallucinations and delusions.

Key terms

Communication passport: *a document that records essential information about the individual and their communication needs and preferences, which should be immediately available to all who provide care for the person*

Community psychiatric nurses (CPNs): *mental health nurses who work in the community, including with people who have dementia-related conditions*

Delusions: *a fixed belief or perception that persists despite evidence to the contrary*

Hallucinations: *seeing things or hearing voices that are not apparent to others*

Interpreter: *a person who translates what is spoken in one language and communicates it in another language*

Speech and language therapists: *specialist practitioners (sometimes referred to by the acronym SALT) who work with individuals with speech, language and communication difficulties*

Transitions: *changing from one situation or environment to another*

- Physiotherapists assist patients with dementia who have motor problems that affect posture and movement, both of which can interfere with communication.

- **Interpreters** will translate for a person with dementia who speaks a different language, including sign language. An interpreter could be a person who is trained to provide a professional service, but can also be a partner, close relative or friend, in which case do consider confidentiality matters before asking for their assistance.

Gathering information together

To form a holistic picture of the best ways to interact with a person with dementia you need to gather information together from a number of sources. These are set out in the diagram below (figure 2.9).

Figure 2.9 Where to find communication information

One useful way of gathering this information together is in the form of a **communication passport**. This is carried by the individual and is particularly useful to support **transitions** between services, helping a new care-provider to communicate effectively with the person and to obtain assessment information about them. Information is recorded in an accessible and person-centred way with a focus on enabling each care provider to work in partnership with the person and their family, as well as with other care practitioners. Creating a communication passport is an ongoing process where information can be added, removed and changed as necessary by anyone involved with the person's care, but

Reflect

Be aware of the content of hand-over meetings and team meetings, such as case conferences where you work . How is information about communication needs, abilities and strengths of individuals with dementia recognised and used to improve communication?

Discuss

Share with colleagues the different knowledge, insights and understanding that can be brought by different members of the care team to enhance communication with individuals with dementia whom you help to support.

Investigate

Spend some time in your work setting observing how your fellow health or social care practitioners communicate with a resident who has dementia. Assess what you think works and doesn't work and identify the person's preferred methods of communication.

always in consultation with, and with the involvement of, the individual. The aims of the communication passport are set out in figure 2.10 below:

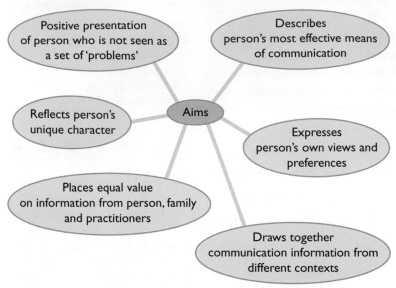

Positive presentation of person who is not seen as a set of 'problems'

Describes person's most effective means of communication

Reflects person's unique character

Aims

Expresses person's own views and preferences

Places equal value on information from person, family and practitioners

Draws together communication information from different contexts

Figure 2.10 The aims of the communication passport

Communication passports commonly take the form of a booklet, but can also be displayed as a wallchart or placemat. They should include information such as:

- work, hobbies and interests

- life story, including special events and important people

- **emotional and behavioural triggers**

- preferences and dislikes – for food, clothing and so on

- impact of sight, hearing or speech difficulties

- the best ways to facilitate communication.

 Key term

Emotional/behavioural triggers: topics, or ways of behaving, that cause an upset or angry response

 Reflect

Do you know whether each individual with dementia whom you provide care for wears spectacles and whether these are for close work, long distance, or bi- or vari-focal to suit both needs? Do they have a hearing aid and is this in good working order? Do regular check-ups with an optician and an audiologist take place?

 Discuss

Share with colleagues your ideas for a communication passport design. Decide on the outward look of it and the features you would include.

Investigate

Using work, library and internet sources, find out more about communication passports, such as by looking at www. communicationpassports.org.uk

Using information to enhance interaction

Make sure you use the information that has been gathered and encourage other staff members in the team to do the same, being aware of what works well for each person and what should be avoided. The following checklist (figure 2.11) should help you remember to apply the information you have gathered to enhance your interactions:

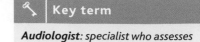

Key term

Audiologist: specialist who assesses hearing and balance disorders

Figure 2.11 Communication information checklist

Aspect of communication	Notes	✓
Awareness of visual/hearing impairment	If a person has a sensory impairment, check that: • audiologist and optician appointments are up to date • hearing aids have batteries • hearing aid set at the correct volume for the person • their ear canal is not full of wax • their spectacles fit comfortably • spectacle lenses are clean.	
Awareness of current issues	Every day can bring new pleasures and challenges, and you need to be up to date with how things are for each person. Check that they: • are feeling well physically and mentally • are not in pain • have had good or bad news • slept well the night before.	
Awareness of personal information	Know about those things that are unique to each person: • familiar words for specific items or people that the person will recognise • avoid topics that cause distress, remembering that memory of past events may remain intact.	
Awareness of personal comfort	Make sure the person is: • in a comfortable position • sufficiently supported in their chair or bed • not too cold or hot/hungry or thirsty • in a good enough light to see.	

Case study

Senga and her husband Scotty both have dementia and are supported by their daughter Annie who lives next door to them. Annie is going into hospital for a routine operation and has contacted the GP, who has known the family for years, and social services, who helped a year ago when she went on holiday, to find out what support will be available for her parents while she is away. Senga has very little short-term memory, but her social skills are extremely well preserved. She loves to have people round for 'a brew' as she calls a cup of tea, but gets most annoyed if anyone other than their cleaner, whom she calls 'our treasure', tries to help her with this – 'interfering', as she says! Scotty never has much conversation, except if you get him going on the subject of fishing, about which he is extremely knowledgeable. He often looks as if he is nodding off to sleep, but actually he's rather deaf and this is his way of getting out of his wife's sociable chit chat, which he finds hard to follow.

1. What different people might have valuable information about how best to support Senga and Scotty?

2. Identify the information you have gathered so far that gives clues about how to enhance interaction with Senga and Scotty.

3. What other information do you need to find out about and who might you ask?

 Reflect

If you were to produce a communication passport for yourself, what sorts of information would it be most important for you to include? Consider why some choices are more important than others for you. Try to apply this understanding to your work with individuals with dementia.

 Discuss

Share with colleagues your experiences of working with an older person whose communication has been disrupted by having dementia. Discuss those interventions and approaches that worked best to establish good communication and positive interactions.

 Investigate

Using work, library and internet sources, find out about the role of the speech and language therapist, occupational therapist and physiotherapist in relation to enhancing communication for individuals with dementia.

Knowledge Assessment Task

This assessment task covers DEM 205 3.3.

There is often a network of different people involved in giving care and support to a person with dementia. To complete this task you need to create a poster that explains the different ways in which involving others may enhance interaction with a person with dementia.

Keep the written work that you produce for this activity as evidence towards your assessment. Your assessor may also want to ask you questions about the way you communicate with individuals with dementia in the work setting.

Practical Assessment Task

This assessment task covers DEM 210 1.2, 1.3.

Communication with a person with dementia can be enhanced by using information gathered from different sources about their communication strengths, abilities, needs and preferred methods of communication. To complete this task you need to:

1. *focus on a person with dementia for whom you provide care*

2. *produce a communication passport that*

    • *gathers information from sources relevant to the person's care*

    • *identifies communication strengths and abilities*

    • *identifies communication needs and preferences.*

Your evidence for this task must be based on your practice and experience in a real work environment.

Assessment checklist

The assessment of this unit is partly knowledge-based (assessing things you need to know about) and partly competence-based (assessing things you need to do in the real work environment). To complete this unit successfully, you will need to produce evidence of both your knowledge and your competence.

The knowledge-based assessment criteria for DEM 205 are listed in the 'What you need to know' table below. The practical or competence-based criteria for DEM 210 are listed in the 'What you need to do' table opposite. Your tutor or assessor will help you to prepare for your assessment, and the tasks suggested in the chapter will help you to create the evidence you need.

Assessment criteria	What you need to know	Assessment task
DEM 205		
1.1	Explain how dementia may influence an individual's ability to communicate and interact	Page 58
1.2	Identify other factors that may influence an individual's ability to communicate and interact	Page 58
1.3	Outline how memory impairment may affect the ability of an individual with dementia to use verbal language	Page 58
2.1	Explain how to identify the communication strengths and abilities of an individual with dementia	Page 64
2.2	Describe how to adapt the style of communication to meet the needs, strengths and abilities of an individual with dementia	Page 70
2.3	Describe how information about an individual's preferred methods of communication can be used to reinforce identity and uniqueness	Pages 64 and 70
3.1	Explain how understanding about an individual's biography/history can facilitate positive interactions	Page 64
3.2	List different techniques that can be used to facilitate positive interactions with an individual with dementia	Page 70
3.3	Explain how involving others may enhance interaction with an individual with dementia	Page 77

Assessment criteria	What you need to do	Assessment task
DEM 210		
1.1	Describe how memory impairment can affect the ability of an individual with dementia to use verbal language	Page 58
1.2	Gather information from others about an individual's preferred methods of communicating to enhance interaction	Page 77
1.3	Use information about the communication abilities and needs of an individual with dementia to enhance interaction	Page 77
1.4	Use a person-centred approach to enable an individual to use their communication abilities	Page 64
1.5	Demonstrate how interaction is adapted in order to meet the communication needs of an individual with dementia	Page 70
2.1	List different techniques that can be used to facilitate positive interactions with an individual with dementia	Page 70
2.2	Use an individual's biography/history to facilitate positive interactions	Page 64
2.3	Demonstrate how the identity and uniqueness of an individual has been reinforced by using their preferred methods of interacting and communicating	Page 64

3 | Equality, diversity and inclusion in dementia care

DEM 207
LO1 Understand and appreciate the importance of diversity of individuals with dementia

▸ Explain the importance of recognising that individuals with dementia have unique needs and preferences

▸ Describe ways of helping carers and others to understand that an individual with dementia has unique needs and preferences

▸ Explain how values, beliefs and misunderstandings about dementia can affect attitudes towards individuals

DEM 207
LO2 Understand the importance of person-centred approaches in the care and support of individuals with dementia

▸ Describe how an individual may feel valued, included and able to engage in daily life

▸ Describe how individuals with dementia may feel excluded

▸ Explain the importance of including the individual in all aspects of their care

DEM 207
LO3 Understand ways of working with a range of individuals who have dementia to ensure diverse needs are met

▸ Describe how the experience of an older individual with dementia may be different from the experience of a younger individual with dementia

▸ Describe what steps might be taken to gain knowledge and understanding of the needs and preferences of individuals with dementia from different ethnic origins

▸ Describe what knowledge and understanding would be required to work in a person centred way with an individual with learning disability and dementia

DEM 209
LO1 Understand the importance of equality, diversity and inclusion when working with individuals with dementia

▶ Explain what is meant by:
  • diversity
  • equality
  • inclusion

▶ Explain why an individual with dementia has unique needs and preferences

▶ Describe how an individual with dementia may feel excluded

▶ Describe why it is important to include an individual with dementia in all aspects of care practice

▶ Explain how values, beliefs and misunderstandings about dementia can affect attitudes towards an individual

DEM 209
LO2 Be able to apply a person centred approach in the care and support of individuals with dementia

▶ Demonstrate how an individual with dementia has been valued, included and able to engage in daily life

▶ Show how an individual's life history and culture has been taken into consideration to meet their needs

▶ Demonstrate how the stage of dementia of an individual has been taken into account when meeting their needs and preferences

▶ Demonstrate ways of helping carers and others to understand that an individual with dementia has unique needs and preferences

DEM 209
LO3 Be able to work with a range of individuals who have dementia to ensure diverse needs are met

▶ Demonstrate how to work in ways that ensure that the needs and preferences of individuals with dementia from a diverse range of backgrounds are met

▶ Describe how the experience of an older individual with dementia may be different from the experience of a younger individual with dementia

▶ Describe how to use a person-centred approach with an individual with a learning disability and dementia

DEM 211
LO1 Understand key legislation and agreed ways of working that ensure the fulfilment of rights and choices of individuals with dementia while minimising risk of harm

▶ Outline key legislation that relates to the fulfilment of rights and choices and the minimising of risk of harm for an individual with dementia

▶ Describe how agreed ways of working relate to the rights of an individual with dementia

▶ Explain why it is important not to assume that an individual with dementia cannot make their own decisions

▶ Explain how the best interests of an individual with dementia must be included when planning and delivering care and support

▶ Explain what is meant by providing care and support to an individual with dementia in the least restrictive way

DEM 211
LO2 Understand how to maintain the right to privacy, dignity and respect when supporting individuals with dementia

▶ Describe how to maintain privacy when providing personal support for intimate care to an individual with dementia

▶ Give examples of how to show respect for the physical space of an individual with dementia

▶ Give examples of how to show respect for the social and emotional space of an individual with dementia

▶ Describe how to use an awareness of the life history and culture of an individual with dementia to maintain their dignity

▶ Outline the benefits of knowing about the past and present interests and life skills of an individual with dementia

DEM 211
LO3 Be able to support individuals with dementia to achieve their potential

▶ Demonstrate how the physical environment may enable an individual with dementia to achieve their potential

▶ Demonstrate how the social environment may enable an individual with dementia to achieve their potential

▶ Support an individual with dementia to use their abilities during personal care activities

▶ Explain how the attitudes of others may enable an individual with dementia to achieve their potential

DEM 211
LO4 Be able to work with carers who are caring for individuals with dementia

▶ Identify some of the anxieties common to carers of an individual with dementia

▶ Outline the legal rights of the carer in relation to an individual with dementia

▶ Involve carers in planning support that enables the rights and choices and protect an individual with dementia from harm

▶ Describe how the need of carers and others to protect an individual from harm may prevent the individual from exercising their rights and choices

▶ Demonstrate how a carer can be supported to enable an individual with dementia to achieve their potential

Case study

Ahmad Mohammed is 76 years of age. He came to the United Kingdom as a refugee fifteen years ago. He is a well-known member of the local Somali community but has no immediate family living in this country. Most members of his family were killed during the civil war in Somalia, causing him to leave for his own safety. Ahmad is able to speak English but is becoming confused and forgetful as a result of a dementia-based condition. He can wash, dress and feed himself but is frightened of leaving the residential home where he has lived for the last two years. A small number of the care workers at the residential home believe that it is not the right place for Ahmad because he 'doesn't fit in' and has 'strange habits'. Ahmad is a practising Muslim and is visited by a small number of Somali friends who sometimes bring him food and take him to a local mosque for Friday prayers.

1. How does the concept of diversity help the people looking after Ahmad to understand his needs?

2. Why is it important for all the care workers to understand and apply the concept of equality when working with Ahmad?

3. What could care workers do to acknowledge and recognise Ahmad's cultural heritage and personal beliefs?

 Investigate

How is diversity acknowledged and celebrated in the care setting where you work or where you are on placement? Find out about the ways in which a person's background, abilities and achievements are assessed and documented, for example. You might also think about the ways in which care workers talk to the people they care for and support, and the ways they talk about them to others.

Inclusion

Dementia care workers and the services they are employed in must promote **inclusion** in order to offer equality of opportunity to those they provide care and support for.

An inclusive dementia care service works hard at:

- identifying and removing barriers to access and participation

- enabling people to use the full range of services and facilities available

- welcoming, valuing and supporting everyone who uses the care setting.

Inclusion doesn't happen by chance. The people who work in a dementia care setting have to:

- be honest and reflective about how their workplace operates

- be critical in a constructive way, so that positive changes can be made

- work at identifying *actual* barriers to access and participation

- remain alert to *potential* barriers that may exclude some people

- act in practical ways to remove actual and potential barriers

- place the individuals who need care at the centre of care planning and practice.

Key term

Inclusion: the process of ensuring that all members of society have access to available services and activities

Reflect

Think about the individuals with dementia for whom you provide care and support. How diverse is this group of people? How do you acknowledge and respond to diversity in the way that you practise at the moment?

Knowledge Assessment Task

This assessment task covers DEM 209 1.1.

With reference to your own care practice and the organisation where you work:

1. *explain what you understand by the concepts of diversity, equality and inclusion*

2. *give an example of the way in which each of these concepts applies to your own care practice.*

Keep your written work as evidence towards your assessment.

Attitudes and beliefs about dementia

Attitudes to dementia

A dementia-based condition will eventually remove a person's **cognitive** capacity, sense of self, ability to control their body functions and dignity. People who may once have been resourceful and competent tend to experience severe memory loss, personality changes, confusion and gradual psychological disintegration as a result of dementia-based conditions. From a **biomedical** perspective, individuals with dementia are seen as sharing a similar set of symptoms and a similar bleak fate because of the way in which a dementia-based condition affects their brain.

Dementia is a **degenerative** condition. There is no cure or effective treatment to stop its destructive effects at present. As a result, and because of the way dementia-based conditions destroy a person's mental and physical capabilities, many people fear it, develop very negative attitudes towards dementia and devalue those who experience it.

Dementia care in the past

Negative attitudes to dementia were very common in health and social care settings in the past. This was partly because health and social care workers didn't focus on the person with the diagnosis of dementia. Instead, they tended to focus on the destructive effects of dementia-based conditions and on the things that people could no longer do. Carers who saw their loved ones losing their abilities and deteriorating before their eyes also tended to focus on the individual's problems and the losses that dementia causes. This kind of approach caused those providing care to dwell on how an individual with dementia used to be, not on what the person could still do or on how they could be stimulated to enjoy life and use the skills and abilities that they still had.

Devaluing people with dementia

There is some truth in seeing dementia as a destructive, incurable condition that is disabling and life-limiting. In the past this led to individuals with dementia being written off and devalued as people, as though their lives were already over. Before the development of the person-centred approach, an individual with dementia was generally viewed as having become 'dysfunctional', 'wrong' (especially in terms of their speech and thinking) and less than the person they once were.

Your assessment criteria:

DEM 209

1.3 Describe how an individual with dementia may feel excluded.

1.4 Describe why it is important to include an individual with dementia in all aspects of care practice.

1.5 Explain how values, beliefs and misunderstandings about dementia can affect attitudes towards an individual (see also DEM 207 1.3).

Key terms

Biomedical: based on a scientific, biological understanding of health and illness

Cognitive: a term used to refer to mental processes such as thinking and memory

Degenerative: gradual and irreversible worsening or deterioration over time.

Investigate

Was there an old-style mental asylum or psychogeriatric hospital in your local area in the past? What was this called and what kind of reputation did it have with local people? You could find out by asking older family members, friends, colleagues or neighbours who have lived in the area for a long time. Try to get a sense of the attitudes people have towards the institution and those who received care there.

The devaluing of people with dementia sometimes led to negative attitudes and impersonal approaches to care. When this happened the person with the dementia was forgotten. What became important were tasks (washing, dressing, feeding, toileting) to overcome the problems caused by dementia. Building relationships, spending time talking, comforting or communicating non-verbally and giving individuals choices about their care were not part of this approach.

The service response to dementia in the past was to provide care in big geriatric or mental hospitals. This was a dead-end world of unstimulating wards with low levels of care staff and often poor standards of care. The lack of stimulating care environments was mirrored by the lack of individualised, imaginative care. It was common for task-focused, 'batch care' methods to be used in these settings. For example, one nurse or care assistant would be required to feed five or six patients at a time. The way in which care was organised and delivered focused on the efficient use of staff time rather than on the needs of individuals with dementia. This undermined the independence, individuality, abilities and self-esteem of those who were subject to these care regimes. The outcome was **institutionalisation**, dependency, more aggressive behaviour, loss of motivation and personality changes. In the past, while a biomedical model informed health and social care workers' understanding of dementia, it failed to provide a way of responding to the care or support needs of the individuals with dementia. The person-centred approach to care does this much more effectively.

? Reflect

Is the task-focused approach to care still used in your workplace or is it something that is avoided? Think about your own practice as well as the general approach used in your workplace.

✎ Key term

Institutionalisation: the loss of initiative and self-care skills that can happen when a person spends a long time in a care home or other institutional setting.

Developing positive attitudes to dementia care

Health and social care workers employed in dementia care settings need to know about and understand the physical impact that dementia as a condition can have on people. However, it is vital that a health or social care worker appreciates that a person with dementia is a whole person and that their job is to understand who they are and how their needs and wishes can best be met. This means being able to see beyond a person's diagnosis of dementia in order to provide appropriate, compassionate and effective care and support for them as an individual. To do this, health and social care workers need to be inclusive in thinking about each individual's gender, ethnicity, sexuality, social class, work and personal background as well as about their particular personality characteristics, individual needs, wishes and preferences. The focus of dementia care practice should be on the *person* with care or support needs – not their dementia-based condition.

Including the individual with dementia

Including individuals with dementia in activities and supporting them to participate in meeting their care needs as much as possible is part of a positive approach to dementia care. Focusing on an individual's wishes and preferences and adopting a strengths-based approach that values and uses the skills they retain is an indicator of a positive, more inclusive approach to care practice.

? Reflect

Think about the words and phrases that are associated with 'dementia care'. Make a list of the things that come to mind when you think about this. Are these words or phrases generally positive or negative? What do your family, friends and colleagues think dementia care involves?

Case study

Sandra, aged 75, lives in a nursing care home. She cannot recall the names or remember the faces of the health and social care workers she sees every day. Sandra doesn't realise that she has dementia or that she is unable to meet her basic personal care needs.

Sandra generally communicates though her behaviour rather than through speech. She does still understand simple language but becomes angry and uncooperative when care workers start to undress or wash her without first explaining. Sandra will hit out at the care worker if they carry on in these circumstances.

1. Identify two reasons why it is important to include Sandra in all aspects of the care and support she requires.

2. What kind of attitudes are being expressed by care workers who don't consult or include Sandra in the care process?

3. Describe two ways of including Sandra in meeting her personal care needs.

? Reflect

Are individuals with dementia consulted about their wishes and preferences in relation to care and support where you work? Is this something that you do as part of your care practice?

Health and social care workers should be able to reflect on the assumptions they make about dementia and on their values and beliefs about people – particularly those with dementia – in order to develop and maintain positive attitudes and a positive approach to dementia care practice.

Knowledge Assessment Task

This assessment task covers DEM 207 1.3 and DEM 209 1.3, 1.4, 1.5, 3.1.

Dementia, and those who experience this condition, are often treated in a negative, devalued way. Reflecting on your own practice and experience of dementia care work:

1. *describe how an individual with dementia may feel excluded in daily living or care situations*

2. *describe why it is important to include an individual with dementia in all aspects of care practice that affect them*

3. *explain how values, beliefs and misunderstandings about dementia can affect attitudes towards an individual.*

Keep your written work as evidence towards your assessment.

Diverse experiences in dementia care

Diversity makes a difference

As a health or social care worker you may already know that it is never a good idea to assume that because a group of people have one thing in common (such as their age or a diagnosis of dementia) they will have other things in common too. This is known as **stereotyping**. Stereotypical assumptions about people with dementia can lead to care practices that are insensitive and inappropriate. Treating everybody as though they are the same – because they have dementia – regardless of their individual needs, wishes, preferences and identities doesn't recognise individuality or acknowledge the importance of diversity. Understanding diversity is key to avoiding insensitive, outdated approaches to care practice.

Diversity refers to the differences that exist between people. Differences relating to age, ethnicity and learning disability can make a difference to an individual's dementia care needs, their experiences of dementia and to their preferences for how they want to receive care and support.

Younger people with dementia

Dementia-based illnesses are generally associated with older people over the age of 65. However, the Alzheimer's Society estimates that there are at least 16,000 people under the age of 65 living with dementia in the United Kingdom today. This group of people often struggle to have their symptoms and problems recognised, and may be misdiagnosed as having depression or stress by medical practitioners who associate dementia with much older people.

Your assessment criteria:

DEM 207

3.1 Describe how the experience of an older individual with dementia may be different from the experience of a younger individual with dementia.

3.2 Describe what steps might be taken to gain knowledge and understanding of the needs and preferences of individuals with dementia from different ethnic origins.

3.3 Describe what knowledge and understanding would be required to work in a person-centred way with an individual with learning disability and dementia.

DEM 209

3.1 Demonstrate how to work in ways that ensure that the needs and preferences of individuals with dementia from a diverse range of backgrounds are met.

3.2 Describe how the experience of an older individual with dementia may be different from the experience of a younger individual with dementia.

3.3 Describe how to use a person-centred approach with an individual with a learning disability and dementia.

🔨 Key term

Stereotyping: ill-informed, exaggerated and often prejudiced ways of thinking about a group of people

Despite the early age of onset, younger people who develop dementia-based conditions experience the same symptoms of memory loss, confusion and disorientation as older people. However, the care and support needs and problems that result from these symptoms may be different for younger people. For example, a younger person is more likely to have:

- significant financial commitments

- a job

- young or dependent children

- family responsibilities

- better general physical and mental health.

As a result, the services and facilities provided for people with dementia in a particular area may be unsuitable if they've been planned and are organised with older people in mind. Some dementia care services will also not admit or work with people unless they are 65 years old or more. This can lead to inadequate and inappropriate support for younger people with dementia and their families. While there is now more awareness of the needs of younger people with dementia and a growing number of services for them, provision is still variable and insufficient throughout the UK.

Investigate

Use an Internet search engine to find out more about organisations that work with younger people who have dementia. Young Dementia and the Alzheimer's Society both have information on this area.

Case study

David grew up in the country. He graduated from University with a very good degree and went on to become an accountant. David was always good with numbers, very well organised and popular with the clients he worked with. David became a partner in an accountancy firm and was doing really well until about five years ago. When he was in his late forties things started to happen that worried his wife, Delia, and his work colleagues. David started to have trouble following simple instructions and began to make errors at work. At first colleagues covered up for him. David then began losing weight and behaving erratically. He would go out for a meeting and not return or would call to say he was lost. David was struggling so much that he was persuaded to take an extended holiday from work. Delia did her best to support David and was extremely worried about him. When things reached the point where David just couldn't look after himself, he was admitted to a mental health unit for assessment. Not long afterwards, he was diagnosed with early onset dementia. He was 54 years of age.

1. How would you feel about working with a younger person with dementia, such as David?

2. How do David's support needs differ from those of an older person?

3. What, if anything, could be offered to David and his family by the care organisation where you work or by local dementia care organisations in your area?

Investigate

What services or forms of support are available for younger people with dementia in your local area? Find out where people would be referred to locally and what information, support or services are provided by your own care organisation (if any).

This assessment task covers DEM 207 3.1 and DEM 209 3.2.

Using the internet, library resources or contacts in your local area or workplace, investigate how developing a dementia-based condition impacts on the life of an older person and a younger person. Using the information you obtain, describe how the experience of an older individual with dementia may be different from the experience of a younger individual with dementia.

Keep your written work as evidence towards your assessment.

Dementia and ethnicity

Individuals with dementia may come from any ethnic group and may have a cultural or religious background that is important to their sense of identity. The Alzheimer's Society estimates that there are about 11,000 people from black and minority ethnic (BME) groups with dementia in the United Kingdom. Approximately 6% of this group are younger people with early onset dementia. Services for people with dementia from BME communities can be inappropriate and inaccessible where cultural identities, beliefs and traditions as well as language differences are not catered for. To avoid this, health and social care workers should find out about each individual's background and values and about the rules, beliefs, customs and traditions that are part of this. To practise in a respectful and sensitive way you will need to know how a person's cultural or religious values and background affect:

- what they can eat

- how they (and others) should dress

- ways of undressing

- personal care issues

- what they feel about physical contact and being touched by others.

Dementia care services do tend to adapt to the needs of people from BME backgrounds where there is a significant local community of BME people. This is more likely to be the case in larger cities than in towns or villages. Outside of major cities, services for people with dementia from BME backgrounds may not be seen as accessible or appropriate ways of meeting their particular needs.

? Reflect

How ethnically diverse is your local area? Does your care setting provide culturally appropriate care for members of the different ethnic groups in your local area? If not, how do you think this might be improved?

Knowledge Assessment Task

This assessment task covers DEM 207 3.2.

In this activity you are required to create an annotated diagram or poster that describes the steps that could be taken to find out about the needs and preferences of individuals with dementia from different ethnic origins. Think about different sources of information, the communication and other skills you might need to use and how you might work with an individual or their family to gain this understanding.

Keep your written work as evidence towards your assessment.

 Key term

Learning disability: a reduced intellectual ability and difficulty with everyday activities

Learning disability and dementia

Learning disabilities can be caused by genetic disorders, such as Down's syndrome, by brain injuries or by pre- or post-natal infections, for example. A learning disability is not an illness but it will affect a person's ability to cope with everyday activities throughout their life.

People with learning disabilities are not typically associated with dementia. However, members of this group are at greater risk of developing dementia than non-learning disabled people. Individuals who have Down's syndrome are at particular risk. Prasher's (1995) research indicates that the older a person with learning disabilities is, the greater their risk of developing dementia.

Dementia affects learning disabled people in much the same way as it affects non-learning disabled people. However, the onset of dementia may be more difficult to detect and diagnose in learning disabled individuals. This is linked to the reduced communication ability learning disabled people tend to have.

For example, an individual with learning disabilities may struggle to express how their abilities have deteriorated. They may not be able to explain their feelings of confusion, disorientation or difficulties with recall very clearly if they have limited verbal skills and vocabulary.

Close family members, carers or health and social care workers who are in close contact with the individual are likely to be the first to notice the kind of changes in a person's behaviour or personality that are symptoms of dementia.

Supporting learning disabled people

People with learning disabilities who develop dementia-based illnesses are best supported through a person-centred approach that focuses on their strengths, the skills and abilities they retain and on their interests. Health and social care workers should promote the independence and quality of life of learning disabled people with dementia while minimising risk.

In particular, it is important to:

- encourage the person to use both verbal and non-verbal ways of expressing their thoughts and feelings

- give the person plenty of time and reassurance, listening actively and carefully to their verbal and non-verbal communication

- support the person to manage their activities of daily life without taking over or doing too much in a way that is deskilling or undermining

- establish and reinforce clear activities of daily living routines to help the person to meet their own needs and feel confident about self-care

- use visual labels and images – as well as non-verbal communication – to help the person communicate and find their way around their home or care environment

- try to ensure that the person's living environment is quiet, calm and relaxed to prevent disturbance and minimise aggressive behaviour.

Case study

Elizabeth is 46 years old and has Down's syndrome. She lives independently in a supported housing flat and managed to look after herself, with occasional support from community workers, until a year ago. Elizabeth fell in the bathroom of her flat while having a shower, breaking her wrist and bruising her ribs. Elizabeth's self-confidence declined markedly after this incident.

During a weekend stay at a specialist care home, staff noticed that Elizabeth was easily confused by what was going on around her. Following a full mental health and physical assessment, Elizabeth was diagnosed as having dementia, probably Alzheimer's disease. The psychiatric team diagnosing her felt that she had probably had the condition for some time.

1. What factors may have made it difficult to diagnose Elizabeth's dementia-based condition?

2. Which features of learning disability would care workers need to take into account when supporting or providing care for Elizabeth?

3. Should Elizabeth be supported to carry on living independently in her flat or do you think this would now be inadvisable?

Knowledge Assessment Task

This assessment task covers DEM 209 3.3 and DEM 207 3.3.

Would you or your workplace colleagues know how to provide appropriate care and support for an individual with a learning disability and dementia if this was required? In this activity you are asked to:

1. *describe the knowledge and understanding that would be required to work in a person-centred way with an individual with a learning disability and dementia*

2. *describe how to use a person-centred approach with an individual with a learning disability and dementia.*

Keep your written work as evidence towards your assessment.

Person-centred dementia care and support

Unique needs and preferences

Health and social care workers should always provide care and support that meets the unique needs and preferences of each individual they work with. The **person-centred approach** to dementia care does this by:

- acknowledging and respecting the diversity of people with dementia

- ensuring that each person is treated equally and fairly

- including individuals in all aspects of care practice and daily life.

Person centred care has been an important means of tackling negative attitudes to dementia and of responding positively to diversity, equality and inclusion issues in dementia care. The person centred approach emphasises that people with dementia should always feel respected and valued by others. Despite having a degenerative condition, a person living with dementia is (and always will be) a unique and valuable human being. Finding ways of making each individual feel valued, included and able to engage in daily life is a central part of your role as a health and social care worker.

Your use of a person-centred approach is beneficial to individuals who have dementia because it will focus your practice on improving each person's experience of everyday life and will extend their cognitive function.

Recognising individuals' unique needs and preferences

From a person-centred perspective, each person with dementia is a unique individual with their own particular combination of physical, social and psychological characteristics, personality and heritage. An individual's personal background and life experience is also likely to have a direct impact on their care and support needs, wishes and preferences. This is why it is important for health and social care workers to understand the *individual* with dementia as well as their illness. To get to know the person as a unique individual you need to:

- listen to what the person has to tell you

- talk to the person's partner and relatives

- obtain as much information about their current abilities and skills as possible

- use all of this information to understand the person as an individual and to shape the way you work with them.

Your assessment criteria:

DEM 209

1.2 Explain why an individual with dementia has unique needs and preferences.

DEM 207

1.1 Explain the importance of recognising that individuals with dementia have unique needs and preferences.

1.2 Describe ways of helping carers and others to understand that an individual with dementia has unique needs and preferences.

Key term

Person-centred approach: *care that focuses on an individual's particular needs, wishes and preferences*

98

It is essential that health and social care workers get to know who the person they are providing care for is. Careful, **active listening** and observation of an individual will enable you to learn quite a lot about them over time. Even those people with limited ability to hold a conversation may be able to indicate non-verbally their likes and dislikes or the things that interest them. An individual's partner, relatives or close friends may also be able to provide you with valuable information about the person's history, past and current interests as well as their particular likes and dislikes.

Taking life history and culture into account

Person-centred care requires an understanding of an individual's life history and cultural background. This involves obtaining personal information from and about the person, prompting them to recall past experiences and understanding their cultural needs. A health or social care worker may have to ask other family members, the person's partner or their carers to respond to some of the questions asked about life history and culture. It may be best to obtain the information over a period of several weeks in order to gain a whole picture of the person's life. The information may relate to a person's:

- lifestyle including their personal habits, such as preferences for tea, coffee, alcohol and whether the person smoked, for example

- diet including food preferences, any special diets, and foods eaten or avoided because of cultural background or religious beliefs, for example

- sleep pattern including any sleeping difficulties, preferred times of going to bed and getting up and any sleep-related medication taken, for example

Key term

Active listening: paying close attention to what a person is saying as well as their non-verbal communication

Reflect

Are you currently using a person-centred approach in your care practice? If not, how could you change your approach so that it is more person centred?

Reflect

How do you find out about the likes and dislikes, interests and life history of the individuals you support and care for?

- personal care needs and preferences, including those related to personal hygiene, dressing, any difficulties in eating and drinking or elimination patterns, for example
- daily living needs, including those relating to home environment, shopping, cooking meals, mobility or managing housework and finances, for example.

The health or social care worker should try to learn about the individual's childhood, family life, school and job history, as well as their views on life, and should be able to build a mental picture of the individual as a person with a rich life history.

 Discuss

Talk to a work or class colleague about their strategies for obtaining information about the life histories of the people they care for and support. Share ideas about ways of obtaining this and how you manage confidentiality issues.

Case study

Brendan is an 84-year-old man with dementia. He is physically fit, but struggles to communicate verbally. Brendan is happiest when moving about. He constantly walks the corridors of the nursing home where he now lives. Some of the other residents find this disturbing and shout at him to sit down.

Brendan can become quite distressed when this happens, and can get very agitated (and even aggressive) if anyone tries to make him to sit down. Brendan waits by the front door of the home and tries to slip out when it is opened. As a result he regularly goes missing. He is always found walking in the nearby park.

The new manager has asked Jo to become Brendan's key worker. Because little is known about his personal history, Jo arranged a meeting with Brendan, his wife and his son to find out more about him. Jo discovered that before he retired, Brendan had been a postman for twenty years. He was also a keen cyclist and a prize-winning gardener. Roses were his special interest.

Brendan's son also told Jo that he was researching their family tree so Jo talked to him about putting together a life story book that could be used to help Brendan remember and to encourage him to communicate. Brendan's family are keen to help with this.

1. How do you think Brendan's personal history may be influencing his current behaviour?

2. How could you use Brendan's interests and likes to plan his day-to-day activities?

3. How do you think a better understanding of Brendan's life history could enable care workers to improve the quality of his life?

Helping others to understand an individual's unique needs and preferences

It is important that everybody caring for an individual with dementia focuses on the person's particular needs and preferences. This includes the person's relatives and friends as well as other professionals. Those close to the individual with dementia or who work regularly with them are likely to be pleased and reassured if you are asking them questions or are seeking information about the person. This is an indication that you are trying to understand the person's particular needs and preferences. You can use the information that you obtain and your understanding of the person to:

- inform and educate colleagues and others who have professional contact with the person about the individual's particular care needs, wishes and preferences

- share ideas, approaches and information with carers and others close to the person to enable them to provide care and support for the individual at home or to include them in care-giving in a residential or in-patient setting.

The relatives and friends of carers need to understand the experiences that the individual is having, and should also be aware of the care needs and preferences of the person. It is helpful to involve carers in as much of the care planning and delivery process as possible. Many carers may have already acquired care-giving skills and abilities and may have a deep knowledge of the individual with dementia. Establishing an effective relationship with a carer is an important way of sharing knowledge and understanding and of valuing their contribution to meeting the person's care and wellbeing needs.

? Reflect

What could you say to an individual's relatives or friends to get them to realise that they should try always to focus on the individual's particular needs and preferences when providing care or support at home?

Knowledge Assessment Task

This assessment task covers DEM 209 1.2 and DEM 207 1.1, 1.2.

The person-centred approach is a key feature of modern dementia-care practice. In this activity you are required to show that you understand the value of this approach. You should:

1. *explain why an individual with dementia has unique needs and preferences*

2. *explain the importance of recognising that individuals with dementia have unique needs and preferences*

3. *describe how you could help carers and others to understand that an individual with dementia has unique needs and preferences.*

Keep your written work as evidence towards your assessment.

Inclusive approaches to dementia care

Providing person-centred dementia care and support

The person-centred approach has significantly changed dementia care practice over the last 20 years. Person-centred care improves standards of care by focusing on the individual with dementia, not just on the condition they have. The characteristics of person-centred care include:

- a personalised approach to care and support

- recognising and responding to diversity and difference

- promoting equality and inclusion in practice

- ensuring that every person with dementia is treated with dignity and respect.

Valuing people in practice

An individual with dementia should always feel valued as a person. This means valuing the person as they are today – not just valuing who they used to be earlier in life. Health and social care workers can help people with dementia to feel valued by:

- being flexible and tolerant in their approach to providing care and support

DEM 207

2.1 Describe how an individual may feel valued, included and able to engage in daily life.

2.2 Describe how individuals with dementia may feel excluded (see also DEM 209 1.3).

2.3 Explain the importance of including the individual in all aspects of their care.

- including individuals in conversations about or relating to them, never talking over them or as though they are not present

- acknowledging that an individual is trying to communicate even when what they say is difficult or even impossible to follow

- giving each person time to express themselves and to complete tasks, never criticising or telling them off for what they have or haven't been able to do

- providing the minimum level of support or assistance an individual requires so that they can maintain their daily living skills and feel empowered and capable of doing as much for themselves as they are able

- being positive when communicating and affectionate in ways that each individual feels comfortable with

- providing the person with opportunities to be active and involving each person in the kinds of activities they can actively take part in

- using each person's preferred title, name or nickname when communicating with them

- being kind and reassuring and never being offhand, impatient or discourteous

- listening and trying to understand a person's feelings, never brushing off their concerns or worries or dismissing them with 'cheer up' or 'never mind' comments.

By valuing a person with dementia you are recognising and respecting them as a unique individual. As well as focusing on who a person is, this approach acknowledges what a person can still do, seeks to include them in their own care and engages them in daily life. As such you should:

- try to identify tasks or activities a person can succeed at and avoid putting them in situations they can't cope with

- support individuals to complete tasks or activities at their own pace and in the way they prefer

- promote individuals' independence by doing things *with* them rather than *for* them

- promote individuals' sense of achievement and self-worth by enabling them to complete part of a task if they cannot manage it all.

> **? Reflect**
>
> *What do you understand by the term 'inclusive practice'? Do you and your colleagues make a conscious effort to be inclusive in the way that you value and include the individuals you provide care for?*

> **🔑 Key term**
>
> **Empowered**: *enabled to do something*

> **? Reflect**
>
> *What do you do to try to promote the independence and self-worth of the people you provide care and support for? Think about your own practice and reflect on situations where you have, or could have, done this.*

Respecting privacy

Individuals with dementia may require assistance to manage their personal care and hygiene, particularly during the later stages of their dementia. Many people with dementia receive care in residential or institutional settings when this stage is reached.

Despite having moved from living in their own home, people in this situation, regardless of their level of dependency, have a right to privacy. It is important to always knock and wait before entering a person's room, for example. It is also important to consider and protect a person's need for privacy when carrying out personal care activities (see also pages 112–13 for more on this). Being exposed to others in such circumstances can make a person feel humiliated and is very disrespectful.

Offering choice

Providing people with dementia with opportunities to choose and to express their own wishes and preferences is an important part of valuing and respecting them as individuals. As part of your dementia care practice you should:

- always inform and ask the person about anything that concerns or involves them rather than make decisions on their behalf

- provide the person with opportunities to make choices that reflect their own wishes and preferences

- give clear, concise information to explain what you are doing or need to do and explain why

- take note of and respond to the person's verbal and non-verbal reactions to what you are saying or doing

- keep choices simple – offering an either/or choice is less confusing than asking an open-ended question about what the person may like to do. It is best to make it easy for them to say 'yes' or 'no' in response to a choice.

Case study

Gerry is 76 years of age. He lives in a residential care home with nine other residents. The care home is part of a community complex with a café and horticultural centre attached. Gerry is the only resident with a diagnosis of dementia.

Until recently Gerry had been quite independent and able to meet most of his personal care needs. He moved to the residential home to try to overcome his loneliness and feelings of isolation.

Amanda, the manager of the residential home, is now concerned about Gerry's safety inside and outside of the home. She has told the staff to escort Gerry everywhere he goes and to prevent him from going to the café or horticultural centre on his own.

Amanda believes that this is the best way of safeguarding Gerry and minimising the risks that she believes he faces now. Gerry is upset and frustrated by this.

1. What effect will Amanda's decision have on Gerry's rights and choices if the care staff do as she says?

2. What could be done to give Gerry choices and respect his rights while also minimising the risks he faces in daily life?

3. How could care staff at the residential home ensure that Gerry is consulted and included in discussions about the best way to provide him with care and support?

Knowledge Assessment Task

This assessment task covers DEM 207 2.1, 2.2, 2.3.

Health and social care workers need to show understanding of the importance of person-centred approaches in dementia care. In this activity you are required to:

1. *describe how an individual may feel valued, included and able to engage in daily life*

2. *describe how individuals with dementia may feel excluded*

3. *explain the importance of including the individual in all aspects of their care.*

Keep your written work as evidence towards your assessment.

Enabling rights and choices

The rights, choices and best interests of people with dementia should be a major concern for all health and social care workers. Legislation and effective, person-centred care practice are the two main ways of **safeguarding** vulnerable adults such as individuals with dementia.

Legislation to enable rights and choices

Health and social care workers are required to work within a framework of laws, **policies** and **procedures** that set out standards for practice and agreed ways of working in dementia care settings. The purpose of key legislation is to protect and fulfil the rights and choices of individuals with dementia while minimising the risk of harm they may face in community or residential care settings. The key points covered by a range of different laws are summarised in figure 3.2 opposite.

Your assessment criteria:

DEM 211

1.1 Outline key legislation that relates to the fulfilment of rights and choices and the minimising of risk of harm for an individual with dementia.

1.2 Describe how agreed ways of working relate to the rights of an individual with dementia.

1.3 Explain why it is important not to assume that an individual with dementia cannot make their own decisions.

1.4 Explain how the best interests of an individual with dementia must be included when planning and delivering care and support.

1.5 Explain what is meant by providing care and support to an individual with dementia in the least restrictive way.

Key terms

Mental capacity: *the ability to make decisions independently*

Policy: *a plan of action*

Procedure: *a way of doing something*

Safeguarding: *protecting from danger and harm*

Figure 3.2 Key legislation safeguarding individuals with dementia

Legislation	Key points
Human Rights Act 1998	• Gives individuals a range of rights that must normally be respected by health and social care workers (see figure 3.3) • Individuals should be kept informed of their rights, including the right to access legal support if that is required • Individuals' human rights can be overruled by care workers or relatives if the person poses a risk or is incapable of making a decision regarding their own welfare
Mental Capacity Act 2005	• Every adult has the right to make his or her own decisions and is assumed to have the mental capacity to do so unless proved otherwise • Individuals with dementia must be supported to make their own decisions, and must be given all practicable help before it is concluded that they cannot make their own decisions • People have the right to make eccentric or unwise decisions without being judged as lacking in capacity • Decisions made on behalf of an individual without capacity must always be in their best interests • Decisions made or actions taken on behalf of a person who lacks capacity should be the least restrictive intervention in terms of their basic rights and freedoms
Adults with Incapacity (Scotland) Act 2000/2007	• Presumes adults are able to make their own decisions regarding medical care unless proved incapable • Judges an adult incapable if he or she is unable to make decisions, communicate decisions, understand decisions and retain a memory • Allows adults to appoint a welfare attorney to make decisions for them in case their condition deteriorates to the point of being without capacity • Any intervention in the care of an incapacitated adult either by a professional or welfare attorney or guardian must benefit the individual, take account of their wishes and the views of others involved in their care
Mental Health Act 2007	• A person may be admitted to receive care or treatment against their will if mentally disordered • Provides a right of appeal against compulsory admission and protection relating to treatment
Disability Discrimination Act 1995/2005	• Prohibits discrimination against a disabled person, including individuals with dementia • Places a duty on public authorities to promote equality of opportunity for disabled people • Services must make 'reasonable adaptations' to enable disabled people to access and use them

Figure 3.2 (continued)

Legislation	Key points
Safeguarding Vulnerable Groups Act 2006	• Restricts contact between vulnerable adults and those who might harm them • Unsuitable people are barred from working with people with dementia • Employers must check that a person is not barred from working with vulnerable people before employing them • Assessment of suitability to work with vulnerable people should be on-going, not a one-off procedure

Carers (Equal Opportunities) Act 2004	• Gives carers who provide or intend to provide a substantial amount of care on a regular basis the right to an assessment of their needs by a local authority
	
	• Local authorities must take into account:
	
	  – whether the carer works or wishes to work
	
	  – whether the carer is undertaking or wishes to undertake education, training or leisure activities
	
	  – support that can be provided from housing, health and education departments
	
	• Gives carers the right to request flexible working hours from their employer
	
	• Gives carers the right to information regarding the individual, as long as confidentiality is maintained

No Secrets (Adult Protection) is a UK government policy document that also provides guidance to local authorities on developing and implementing policies and procedures to protect vulnerable adults from abuse. The aim of the policy is to develop effective **multi-agency** arrangements for safeguarding adults who are vulnerable to abuse. People with dementia should be covered by these arrangements.

Health and social care workers need to understand how these laws provide a framework for their own care practice. There may also be circumstances where colleagues, carers or others require information and guidance on the rights of an individual with dementia.

 Key terms

Confidentiality: *protecting the privacy of information*

Multi-agency: *an arrangement that involves more than one care agency or organisation working together in a collaborative way*

 Discuss

Which law protects the rights of the individual with dementia in each of the circumstances listed below?

- *A local café owner refuses to serve an individual with dementia because they are 'too messy'.*

- *An individual with dementia complains that her daughter is trying to take control of her bank account and finances.*

- *A nurse wishes to give a man with dementia medication against his will in order to calm the person down.*

- *A residential home is refusing to modify its facilities to enable an individual with dementia to access the garden area in her wheelchair.*

- *Mrs Gee is concerned that one of the new carers who come to her home to support her will hurt her or steal from her.*

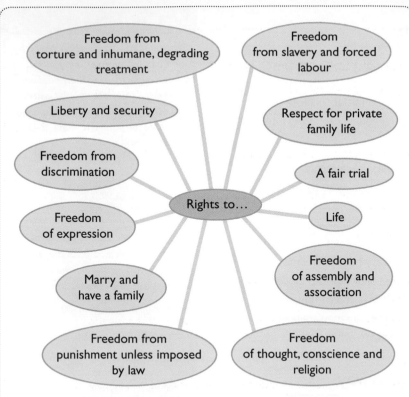

Figure 3.3 Rights protected by the Human Rights Act 1998

Agreed ways of working

Health and social care organisations have a responsibility to ensure that their employees follow the laws safeguarding individuals with dementia in the way they provide dementia care and support. Care organisations do this by producing policies and procedures on agreed ways of working in their care settings. The policies and procedures should incorporate all of the legal requirements affecting care work.

As a result, it is essential that health and social care workers understand and follow these policies and procedures. Failure to follow the agreed ways of working in a care setting may result in a health or social care worker ignoring safe systems of working, not achieving the required standards or objectives of their care organisation and possibly breaking the law and denying an individual with dementia their legal rights.

Investigate

Find out where the policies and procedures used in your workplace are kept and what they say about agreed ways of working in relation to health and safety, confidentiality and moving and handling situations.

? Reflect

Why do you think it is important that every one of your colleagues understands and follows the agreed ways of working in relation to an area of practice such as moving and handling people or objects? What might be the consequences of not doing so?

Recognising mental capacity

Dementia-based illnesses are degenerative conditions. This means that individuals experience a gradual but inevitable loss of brain function. At some point, a person with a dementia-based condition will lose their mental capacity. That is, they will become incapable of making informed judgments and decisions for themselves.

However, despite the likelihood of an individual with dementia losing mental capacity at some point, health and social care workers should not assume that a person with dementia is necessarily incapable of making their own decisions. Many people with dementia remain capable of making choices and of indicating their wishes and preferences until they reach the latter stages of their illness. You should always try to offer an individual choice, support them in expressing their wishes and respect their decisions. It may be necessary at times to adapt the way that you communicate with an individual and to be very sensitive to the way they are able to communicate verbally and non-verbally, in order to achieve this.

Working in the least restrictive way

Many individuals with dementia are, or become vulnerable and dependent. That is, they gradually lose the ability to manage their own safety and meet their own daily living and care needs. Health and social care workers who are aware of risk and the vulnerabilities of the people they work with need to find ways of working that avoid unduly restricting an individual's choices and freedoms. It is always important to manage risk, but at the same time individuals with dementia do have the right to make their own choices and may behave in ways that seem eccentric, irrational or even embarrassing to others. In these circumstances, health and social care workers must respect an individual's rights and find the least restrictive way of providing the care, support and safeguarding the individual requires.

? Reflect

Can you think of a situation in which you demonstrated respect for the mental capacity of an individual with dementia? Think about what you did and why you thought it was important to enable the person to make their own decision.

💬 Discuss

With a colleague, or in a small group, discuss how each of the following workplace policies affects the way that you work with individuals with dementia in your care setting:

- *Moving and handling policy*
- *Confidentiality policy*
- *Equal opportunities policy*
- *Safeguarding policy*
- *Medication management policy*

Case study

Farrah Shamash, aged 84, is a resident at Hinksey House, a residential and nursing care home. Farrah is one of the few residents who has a dementia-based condition.

The staff at Denby House try hard to meet Farrah's needs but complain that there are too few of them and that she needs constant monitoring. Jean, a supervisor, is particularly concerned about Farrah's constant wandering. She believes that this is a health and safety risk, that it upsets other residents and takes up too much staff time to manage.

Jean has started to block the entrance to Farrah's room with a safety gate normally used to stop babies and toddlers from wandering. Farrah can now see out and be seen by staff but can no longer actually leave her room unaided.

1. Explain whether you think Jean's way of managing Farrah's behaviour is reasonable or discriminatory.

2. What impact might Jean's approach to this situation have on Farrah?

3. Describe what you think would be the least restrictive way of responding to Farrah's wandering behaviour.

Knowledge Assessment Task

This assessment task covers DEM 211 1.1, 1.2, 1.3, 1.4, 1.5.

The rights and choices of individuals with dementia are protected by a range of laws and the policies and procedures used in dementia care settings.

In this activity you are required to produce an induction handout for colleagues new to dementia care work in which you:

1. *outline key legislation that relates to the fulfilment of rights and choices and the minimising of risk of harm for an individual with dementia*

2. *describe how agreed ways of working relate to the rights of an individual with dementia*

3. *explain why it is important not to assume that an individual with dementia cannot make their own decisions*

4. *explain what is meant by providing care and support to an individual with dementia in the least restrictive way.*

Keep your written work as evidence towards your assessment.

Maintaining privacy, dignity and respect through care practice

Providing intimate care

Health and social care workers should be able to meet the personal care needs and preferences of individuals with dementia in a supportive and dignified way. This might include assisting a person to:

- use toilet facilities

- bathe, wash and/or manage their mouth care

- dress, undress or manage their personal appearance.

Maintaining privacy when providing intimate care is always an important issue because:

- it affects an individual's dignity and self-respect

- the individual may be vulnerable

- the individual might feel they are a burden.

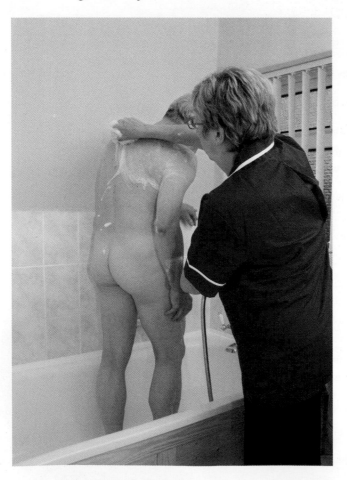

Your assessment criteria:

DEM 211

2.1 Describe how to maintain privacy when providing personal support for intimate care to an individual with dementia.

DEM 209

2.1 Demonstrate how an individual with dementia has been valued, included and able to engage in daily life.

2.3 Demonstrate how the stage of dementia of an individual has been taken into account when meeting their needs and preferences.

2.4 Demonstrate ways of helping carers and others to understand that an individual with dementia has unique needs and preferences.

? Reflect

Think of the last time that you provided intimate care for an individual at work. What did you do to protect their dignity and to show them respect?

Health and social care workers need to:

- understand how individuals might feel in this kind of situation

- show respect for and sensitivity towards the person

- protect the individual's dignity when providing care.

How can privacy be maintained?

Individuals should always have privacy when personal care is being provided. When washing, dressing, bathing, or attending to other personal care needs, they should always be out of sight and – if possible – out of earshot of other people.

How you achieve this should be agreed with the individual and should follow the agreed ways of working for your work setting. Key points include:

- keeping the bathroom or toilet door closed and/or locked

- pulling curtains or a screen around the person's bed

- never leaving the individual partially dressed in view of others

- always knocking before you enter a private area

- talking quietly during care procedures so others can't overhear you.

? Reflect

Reflect on a time when you were involved in a sensitive personal care situation. How did you feel about either providing or receiving support?

Case study

Sheila has been diagnosed with the early stages of dementia and has recently suffered a stroke. She has lost the ability to speak as a result of her stroke and spends much of the day in a chair. When she wants something she uses flashcards.

The set of flashcards helps her communicate when she is hungry, wants to brush her hair, or for any other issues that are important to her wellbeing and comfort. Stanislas, a care worker, is aware that the flashcards are used by Sheila when she wants to use the toilet.

During the morning Stanislas notices that Sheila is looking at him. He goes over to her and suggests she uses the flashcards to say if she wants something. At first Sheila looks embarrassed, but then shows Stanislas the card with a picture of a toilet on it.

Stanislas is about to help take Sheila to the toilet, when he remembers something else. He shows her the card with a picture of a woman on it. Sheila smiles and nods her head.

Stanislas then goes to ask his colleague Maria to help Sheila. When using the toilet, Maria leaves Sheila alone then knocks on the door after a few minutes to see if she is finished, before helping her back to her chair.

1. Why might Sheila be reluctant to tell Stanislas about her personal care needs?

2. How does Stanislas encourage Sheila to communicate her care needs?

3. How does Maria help maintain Sheila's privacy?

Your assessment criteria:

DEM 211

2.2 Give examples of how to show respect for the physical space of an individual with dementia.

2.3 Give examples of how to show respect for the social and emotional space of an individual with dementia.

Respecting personal, social and emotional space

Individuals with dementia may live in their own homes in the community or in residential settings such as nursing and care homes. The place a person lives is usually personalised with pictures, ornaments and items of furniture that have special meaning for the person.

An individual's personal environment, whether it is their own home or their room in a care home, may also give the person a sense of security and feel like somewhere the person can truly be themselves.

Health and social care workers should always respect an individual's need to have such a personal space. The policies and procedures of care settings usually state that care workers should knock and gain permission before entering a person's room and be respectful when working in a person's own home.

 Investigate

What are the causes of a 'stroke'? Use an internet search engine or reference materials to investigate this and the reasons why a person's ability to use and understand speech may be affected.

 Investigate

Investigate how individuals in your work setting are supported with their personal care.

Giving an individual social and emotional space involves respecting emotional involvement with others. Having opportunities to participate in everyday activities, and to make a positive contribution to community and society, helps individuals with dementia to avoid social isolation. At the same time, health and social care workers should also respect the need people have to choose whether or not, and with whom, they wish to socialise or form relationships.

Individuals with dementia may enjoy social contact and activities with others, but should always be given the opportunity to opt out or choose their own company too. It is important to ensure that vulnerable people, such as those with dementia, do not become socially isolated and are not put at risk because of privacy policies and that they are not emotionally manipulated or overwhelmed by the way others behave and relate towards them.

Drawing on life history, culture and skills

Interacting with service users and their families in ways that clearly demonstrate respect is a very important part of inclusive practice in health and social care settings. Everybody who uses your care setting should be valued and respected for who they are, whatever their physical characteristics or their social or cultural background.

People feel respected when you:

- treat them as an equal while recognising their individual needs, wishes and preferences

- acknowledge and recognise that their beliefs, culture and traditions are an important part of who they are

- use inclusive, non-discriminatory language that avoids stereotypes, prejudices and **stigmatised** terms

- are open minded and prepared to discuss their needs, issues and concerns in a way that recognises the unique qualities of each person, as well as the characteristics they share with others

- show interest in their cultural and religious traditions and take part in an appropriate way in celebrating festivals and events that are significant for them and their community.

Using life histories or biographies is a good way of getting to know the individual with dementia and facilitating positive interactions. The aim of the **life history** is to build up a picture of a person's life.

You can do this by asking the person questions about their past life experiences or use familiar artefacts – for example, photographs, pictures and favourite music – to stimulate a conversation. Friends, family members and partners can also provide artefacts to fill in the gaps as you try to piece together the individual's history.

If the individual is being admitted to a care home then it is usually acceptable for a family member to bring in some items of furniture – perhaps a favourite ornament or a quilt from the home – to bring a personal touch to the person's immediate surroundings. **Memorabilia** from the individual's previous employment or hobbies should also be encouraged. These can act as prompts to obtain information that would give a good insight into what the person was like before they developed dementia.

Your assessment criteria:

DEM 209

2.2 Show how an individual's life history and culture has been taken into consideration to meet their needs.

DEM 211

2.4 Describe how to use an awareness of the life history and culture of an individual with dementia to maintain their dignity.

2.5 Outline the benefits of knowing about the past and present interests and life skills of an individual with dementia.

Key terms

Life history: an account of an individual's personal history

Memorabilia: objects and items that have a special meaning for a person

Stigmatised: treated with disapproval

Knowledge Assessment Task

This assessment task covers DEM 211 2.1, 2.2, 2.3, 2.4, 2.5.

It is important that you understand how to maintain the right to privacy, dignity and respect when supporting individuals with dementia.

In this activity you are required to reflect on your own care practice and experiences of working in dementia care settings. You should then:

1. *describe how to maintain privacy when providing personal support for intimate care to an individual with dementia*

2. *give examples of how to show respect for the physical space of an individual with dementia*

3. *give examples of how to show respect for the social and emotional space of an individual with dementia*

4. *describe how to use an awareness of the life history and culture of an individual with dementia to maintain their dignity*

5. *outline the benefits of knowing about the past and present interests and life skills of an individual with dementia.*

Keep your written work as evidence towards your assessment.

Practical Assessment Task

This assessment task covers DEM 209 2.1, 2.2, 2.3, 2.4.

Health and social care workers need to demonstrate the ability to use a person-centred approach when caring for and supporting individuals with dementia.

In this activity you are required to use your own care practice to:

1. *demonstrate how an individual with dementia has been valued, included and enabled to engage in daily life*

2. *show how an individual's life history and culture has been taken into consideration to meet their needs*

3. *demonstrate how the stage of dementia of an individual has been taken into account when meeting their needs and preferences*

4. *demonstrate ways of helping carers and others to understand that an individual with dementia has unique needs and preferences.*

Your evidence must be based on your practice in a real work environment and must be witnessed by or be in a format acceptable to your assessor.

Supporting individuals with dementia to achieve their potential

Physical environments and technologies

A person with a dementia-based condition may remain living in their own home, particularly in the early stages of their condition, or may require care and support in a residential setting such as a care home. The physical environment where the person lives and receives care can have an important impact on their experience of the condition and on their ability to maintain and use self-care and everyday living skills. For example, an individual who has, or who develops, a mobility problem may need the environment to be adapted to enable them to move about using walking aids or a wheelchair. A cluttered, poorly lit environment can increase a person's confusion and result in loss of independence and a greater risk of falls, for example. A person's short-term memory problems can also lead to them becoming disorientated and even getting lost in a residential care setting if they are not really familiar with the environment. This might then lead, for example, to continence problems if a person is unable to find the toilet or is concerned about finding one in time.

Your assessment criteria:

DEM 211

3.1 Demonstrate how the physical environment may enable an individual with dementia to achieve their potential.

3.3 Support an individual with dementia to use their abilities during personal care activities.

3.4 Explain how the attitudes of others may enable an individual with dementia to achieve their potential.

People with dementia can be supported to make effective use of the environment where they live through:

- physical adaptation of the environment (for example, use of ramps and stairlifts, use of lighting that doesn't create shadows)

- the use of visual prompts and symbols to identify different areas of the environment and specific rooms (for instance, colour-coded arrows, images or clean signs)

- the use of safety measures (such as safety switches, locks on outside gates, secure storage of household cleaners, removal of hazards)

- the provision and use of **assistive technologies**.

Many assistive technologies are now available to support and enable people with dementia to maintain their quality of life and daily living skills. In some circumstances an individual's use of assistive technologies may delay or prevent their admission to a care home if the technology is appropriate for their needs. **Occupational therapists** can assess an individual's needs in this area and make recommendations or referrals that give access to these technologies.

 Key terms

Assistive technology: *a product or service that enables an individual to live or maintain their independence or be safer*

Occupational therapist: *a registered care professional who assesses a person's functioning and can recommend meaningful activities or forms of support (including equipment) to maintain this*

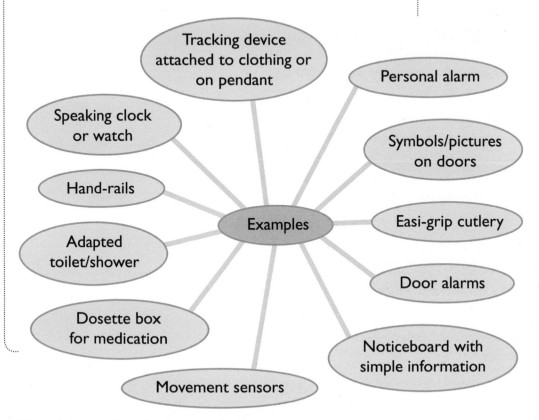

Figure 3.4 Examples of assistive technologies

Health and social care workers can safeguard an individual within their own home or a care setting by accompanying them when they need to move around to complete tasks. It is better to encourage and support the person rather than take over or complete the task for them, even if this is a lot quicker and easier for you to do.

People who don't use their daily living skills quickly lose them when too much care is provided for them in situations like this. Minimising background noise also helps the person to focus on a task or conversation and helps to reduce confusion and unsettling distractions.

Social and emotional environments

A holistic approach to dementia care focuses on the social and emotional environment in which an individual lives as well as the more obvious physical environment. The social relationships that a person has, the network of relatives, friends and others who support them, are a key part of their personal and intellectual life and help them to maintain their links with the community.

Social relationships provide people with opportunities to share activities with others and to express their identity and beliefs and explore their interests. Friends and relatives who care about an individual are likely to support and boost the person's self-esteem by validating the person, offering affection and supporting them to express their feelings.

Health and social care workers can create a supportive social and emotional environment for individuals with dementia through:

- positive verbal and non-verbal communication

- positively reinforcing an individual's efforts and successful attempts to engage in social relationships

- encouraging and assisting a person to take part in physical exercise that also engages them in social activities with others

- providing reminiscence activities that use the person's current skills and that reinforce and validate their social and emotional experiences

- using a range of sensory stimuli to engage individuals in activities that trigger positive emotions

- developing a supportive relationship with and a consistent approach to the way they engage with the individual with dementia.

Your assessment criteria:

DEM 211

3.2 Demonstrate how the social environment may enable an individual with dementia to achieve their potential.

Enabling personal care activities

Effective personal hygiene and care of an individual's appearance should be seen as being part of enabling them to live a healthy lifestyle. An individual with dementia may neglect their personal hygiene because of their short-term memory problems or because disability prevents them from meeting their own personal care needs. This can lead to a loss of social contact and reduced self-esteem for the individual as well as an increased risk of them developing and spreading infections.

Health and social care workers need to be sensitive to an individual's need for privacy, dignity and comfort when dealing with personal care issues. As in other areas of practice, it is best to try to promote an individual's independence and self-care skills so that they can meet as many of their own personal care needs as possible. Diversity issues should also be considered when providing personal care. In particular, it is important to take an individual's religious or cultural beliefs and preferences into account when they require support or direct assistance with personal care.

More frequent support or assistance with personal care needs may be required if an individual is incontinent or has skin problems (such as pressure sores) as these issues raise the risk of infection. Where you do need to support or directly assist an individual with their personal care needs you should adopt the following:

- Find out what kind of help or assistance the person needs and ask them how they would like you to assist them before you begin. Where the person follows a routine that has become familiar to them, follow this to minimise confusion.

- Where the person is unable to communicate their needs clearly, explain the process (what you need to do and how you will do it) as clearly and tactfully as possible.

- Break the personal care activity into a series of easy-to-understand steps and prompt the person to work through each step using simple language.

- Make use of any aids or assistive technologies (such as grab rails, adapted toilets) that can help to promote the individual's independence and self-care skills.

- Use personal protective equipment (for example, gloves and apron) to reduce any infection and cross-infection risks.

- Help the person to set up or organise the washing or dressing situation to promote their independence and respect their right to make choices. It is usually best to provide limited choices to avoid confusion and to set out clothes or equipment in order of use.

- Ensure that you allow the person enough time to carry out any washing, dressing or personal care procedure.

- Monitor the person's safety – and the safety of the environment – throughout any personal care procedure. You should check water temperature, use anti-slip mats and ensure that all equipment is in safe, working order before starting, for example.

- Give as much encouragement to the person as possible and praise them for their efforts and achievements in managing their own personal care needs.

Enabling attitudes

Encouraging a person to manage their own personal care needs and giving praise and positive reinforcement for their efforts to do this is an example of an enabling attitude in action. Enabling attitudes are positive in the sense that they recognise another person's abilities and potential to achieve. This is important in dementia care settings where many individuals may have been treated as though they no longer have any useful abilities and cannot achieve anything for themselves. Health and social care workers who have enabling attitudes may be able to use the relationship they develop with an individual with dementia to raise the person's expectations of what they can still achieve, boosting their sense of self-respect and self-identity. Enabling attitudes that promote an individual's self-belief are more likely to promote a person's sense of independence and use of self-care skills than attitudes based on low expectations and a negative view of the individual with dementia.

Practical Assessment Task

This assessment task covers DEM 211 3.1, 3.2, 3.3, 3.4.

Part of your role as a health or social care worker in a dementia care setting is to support individuals with dementia to achieve their potential. This requires positive attitudes and an enabling approach to each individual. In this activity you are required to show that you can:

1. *demonstrate how the physical environment may enable an individual with dementia to achieve their potential*

2. *demonstrate how the social environment may enable an individual with dementia to achieve their potential*

3. *support an individual with dementia to use their abilities during personal care activities*

4. *explain how the attitudes of others may enable an individual with dementia to achieve their potential.*

Your evidence must be based on your practice in a real work environment and must be witnessed by or be in a format acceptable to your assessor.

Working with carers

Common anxieties of carers

Health and social care workers often provide support for the relatives and friends of individuals with dementia, particularly when the individual first has contact with care services or at points where the person's health or support needs change significantly. A person's main carer may contact a dementia care provider seeking support or enquiring about the services they provide because they have become concerned about:

- the safety or health of the individual with dementia

- the prognosis and life expectancy of the person

- their ability to cope with the demands of providing care and support or worries about failing as a carer

- financial pressures associated with being an unpaid carer

- the effect that caring for an individual with dementia is having on their personal and family relationships.

Health and social care workers should be approachable and be willing to listen to the anxieties that a person's carer may have. Being supportive and helpful in this way may be enough to reduce the carer's stress levels. Health and social care workers are not expected to take on or resolve all of the problems that carers face. Listening and referring people to appropriate sources of information and support, such as local carer support groups, voluntary organisations or other relevant services, can help to alleviate the pressures that many carers experience.

Your assessment criteria:

DEM 211

4.1 Identify some of the anxieties common to carers of an individual with dementia.

4.2 Outline the legal rights of the carer in relation to an individual with dementia.

4.3 Involve carers in planning support that enables the rights and choices and protects an individual with dementia from harm.

4.4 Describe how the need of carers and others to protect an individual from harm may prevent the individual from exercising their rights and choices.

4.5 Demonstrate how a carer can be supported to enable an individual with dementia to achieve their potential.

Key term

Prognosis: a prediction of the likely outcome of an illness

Legal rights of carers

The carers of individuals with dementia have a number of legal rights. These cover issues such as assessment of their own needs as well as financial issues related to providing care for their relative.

- The Carers and Disabled Children Act 2000 says that all carers aged 16 or above, who provide a 'regular and substantial amount of care' for someone aged 18 or over, have the right to an assessment of their needs as a carer.

- The Carers (Equal Opportunities) Act 2004 makes it a legal requirement for all local authorities to ensure that carers are made aware of their right to a carer's needs assessment. The local authority must take a carer's needs and wishes into account when deciding what services to provide for the carer and the person they look after.

Involvement of carers

Every member of a family is likely to be affected by an individual's dementia. The way that family members respond to a person with dementia is likely to depend on the quality of the relationships they had with the person before he or she developed the condition. Many relatives, particularly the partners of individuals with dementia, commit themselves to providing as much care and support for the person as they are able to. This can become stressful and changes the lifestyle of the carer considerably. Health and social care workers can provide support and assistance for carers in a number of ways, including:

- listening to concerns of carers in a genuine and supportive way

- discussing and suggesting safety measures to safeguard both the individual with dementia and the carer

- involving the carer in discussions about the individual's care with other key personnel (doctors, social workers, nurses)

- providing information and guidance on care-related issues through factsheets

- encouraging the carer to promote the independence of their relative and to maintain their own interests and activities outside of caring

- involving the carer in planning support and care for their relative

- discussing and identifying risks to their own and their relative's health and safety

- encouraging the carer to make use of advocates and interpreters where these are required to get the best from care services on behalf of their relative.

Investigate

Using an internet search engine, locate the NHS Choices website and go the Carers Direct section of the site to find out more about the rights carers have to legal, financial and other forms of support.

It is always best not to advise a person's relatives on how they should live their life or what they should do in particular circumstances. A partnership approach in which you provide support and suggestions is more helpful than telling people who are under pressure what they should do. Taking notice of what family members tell you about their relative and the care situation they face and trying to understand their point of view is a useful way of involving carers and is likely to feel reassuring to them.

Restriction of independence

The carers of individuals with dementia don't always have a positive attitude or adopt a person-centred approach to their partner or relative with dementia. Though a person's relatives may act in ways that you do not approve of, it is best not to make assumptions about the reasons or their motives for this. Some relatives may see the individual's dementia as a tragedy they are personally unable to face while others may deny the reality of the impact that the condition is having on their loved one. Often family members are overwhelmed by feelings of sadness and loss and want to protect the person from the impact of their condition as much as possible. This can sometimes lead to situations where partners or relatives become over-involved with providing care and over-protective of their relative. As a result they may:

- prevent the person from having choices or making decisions about even minor aspects of day-to-day living

- over-assess and over-estimate the risks that the person faces in daily life as a result of their dementia

- start to perform personal care tasks or other activities for the individual even though the person is capable of doing this themselves

- restrict the movements of the person in case they get lost or because they fear the person will be unable to cope outside of the home

- start to make decisions for the person and strongly influence the individual's wishes instead of enabling and allowing the person to express their own preferences

- speak for the person when they could do this for themselves.

Supporting carers

The carers of individuals with dementia are often very involved in providing care and support for their partner of relative. It is important to recognise that this is a stressful role to play and that carers may themselves require care and support to cope with the demands this

? Reflect

How do you involve carers in the care and support of their relatives? Think about your recent contact with carers and the extent to which you have formed positive relationships with them.

makes on them. Health and social care workers can make life easier and less stressful for carers by:

- involving them in all aspects of planning support and care for their partner or relative
- forming positive relationships with carers
- treating carers respectfully and working in partnership with them to ensure the individual's needs are met appropriately
- using a person-centred approach that acknowledges and respects the individuality and specific needs and preferences of the person with dementia
- encouraging and supporting the carer so that they allow the individual to have control and make decisions about their own care and daily living activities
- modelling good practice in the way that you communicate with and provide care for individuals with dementia
- providing factsheets and other sources of information on issues concerning carers
- helping the carer to make links to others in carer support groups
- sharing ideas about care provision and suggestions for activities that would engage the individual with dementia.

Case study

Dominic is 66 years old and has a diagnosis of multi infarct dementia. He lives at home with his wife, who is his main carer. Dominic took early retirement eight years ago due to his deteriorating health and difficulties at work. He had worked as a solicitor prior to this. His condition has deteriorated significantly over the past six months and he now requires full care at home. Dominic has 'good days' and 'bad days'. On his good days he is able to say a few words and understands what people say to him. He also likes to watch television and folds clothes. However, on his bad days Dominic is very withdrawn and inactive. He is unable to meet any of his own needs and requires considerable help with tasks like washing, dressing and eating. Dominic is prone to chest infections and has some heart failure. His condition is deteriorating overall and his recent care plan meeting discussed residential care arrangements.

1. Why is it important to assess and take into account Dominic's wife's needs when planning Dominic's care?
2. What impact might Dominic's experience of dementia and his need for constant care have on his wife's physical and mental health?
3. How could appropriate support be provided for Dominic's wife?

People who care for partners and relatives with dementia tend to be very committed to providing high-quality care and support. Most people in this situation will need support and help themselves at some point. This might include help to provide care so that the carer can have some time off or emotional support to express their feelings and concerns about the situation they are dealing with. Health and social care workers can play an important role in enabling carers to acknowledge, look for and obtain the kinds of support they need.

Practical Assessment Task

This assessment task covers DEM 211 4.1, 4.2, 4.3, 4.4, 4.5.

Carers play a vital role in supporting individuals with dementia. Health and social care workers need to understand what it is like to be in the carer's position and should know about the legal rights and resources that are available to help carers. In this activity you are required to:

1. *identify some of the anxieties common to carers of an individual with dementia*

2. *outline the legal rights of the carer in relation to the individual with dementia*

3. *involve carers in planning support that enables the rights and choices and protects an individual with dementia from harm*

4. *describe how the need of carers and others to protect an individual with dementia from harm may prevent the individual from exercising their rights and choices*

5. *demonstrate how a carer can be supported to enable an individual with dementia to achieve their potential.*

Your evidence must be based on your practice in a real work environment and must be witnessed by or be in a format acceptable to your assessor.

Assessment checklist

The assessment of this unit is partly knowledge-based (assessing things you need to know about) and partly competence-based (assessing things you need to do in the real work environment). To complete this unit successfully, you will need to produce evidence of both your knowledge and your competence.

The knowledge-based assessment criteria for DEM 207, DEM 209 and DEM 211 are listed in the 'What you need to know' table below and opposite. The practical or competence-based criteria for DEM 209 and DEM 211 are listed in the 'What you need to do' table on pages 130–1. Your tutor or assessor will help you to prepare for your assessment, and the tasks suggested in the chapter will help you to create the evidence you need.

Assessment criteria	What you need to know	Assessment task
DEM 207		
1.1	Explain the importance of recognising that individuals with dementia have unique needs and preferences	Page 101
1.2	Describe ways of helping carers and others to understand that an individual with dementia has unique needs and preferences	Page 101
1.3	Explain how values, beliefs and misunderstandings about dementia can affect attitudes towards individuals	Page 91
2.1	Describe how an individual may feel valued, included and able to engage in daily life	Page 105
2.2	Describe how individuals with dementia may feel excluded	Page 105
2.3	Explain the importance of including the individual in all aspects of their care	Page 105
3.1	Describe how the experience of an older individual with dementia may be different from the experience of a younger individual with dementia	Page 94
3.2	Describe what steps might be taken to gain knowledge and understanding of the needs and preferences of individuals with dementia from different ethnic origins	Page 95
3.3	Describe what knowledge and understanding would be required to work in a person-centred way with an individual with learning disability and dementia.	Page 97

Assessment criteria	What you need to know	Assessment task
DEM 209		
1.1	Explain what is meant by diversity, equality and inclusion	Page 87
1.2	Explain why an individual with dementia has unique needs and preferences	Page 101
1.3	Describe how an individual with dementia may feel excluded	Page 91
1.4	Describe why it is important to include an individual with dementia in all aspects of care practice	Page 91
1.5	Explain how values, beliefs and misunderstandings about dementia can affect attitudes towards an individual	Page 91
DEM 211		
1.1	Outline key legislation that relates to the fulfilment of rights and choices and the minimising of risk of harm for an individual with dementia	Page 111
1.2	Describe how agreed ways of working relate to the rights of an individual with dementia	Page 111
1.3	Explain why it is important not to assume that an individual with dementia cannot make their own decisions	Page 111
1.4	Explain how the best interests of an individual with dementia must be included when planning and delivering care and support	Page 111
1.5	Explain what is meant by providing care and support to an individual with dementia in the least restrictive way.	Page 111
2.1	Describe how to maintain privacy when providing personal support for intimate care to an individual with dementia	Page 117
2.2	Give examples of how to show respect for the physical space of an individual with dementia	Page 117
2.3	Give examples of how to show respect for the social and emotional space of an individual with dementia	Page 117
2.4	Describe how to use an awareness of the life history and culture of an individual with dementia to maintain their dignity	Page 117
2.5	Outline the benefits of knowing about the past and present interests and life skills of an individual with dementia	Page 117

Assessment criteria	What you need to do	Assessment task
DEM 209		
2.1	Demonstrate how an individual with dementia has been valued, included and able to engage in daily life	Page 117
2.2	Show how an individual's life history and culture has been taken into consideration to meet their needs	Page 117
2.3	Demonstrate how the stage of dementia of an individual has been taken into account when meeting their needs and preferences	Page 117
2.4	Demonstrate ways of helping carers and others to understand that an individual with dementia has unique needs and preferences	Page 117
3.1	Demonstrate how to work in ways that ensure that the needs and preferences of individuals with dementia from a diverse range of backgrounds are met	Page 91
3.2	Describe how the experience of an older individual with dementia may be different from the experience of a younger individual with dementia	Page 94
3.3	Describe how to use a person centred approach with an individual with a learning disability and dementia	Page 97
DEM 211		
3.1	Demonstrate how the physical environment may enable an individual with dementia to achieve their potential	Page 122
3.2	Demonstrate how the social environment may enable an individual with dementia to achieve their potential	Page 122
3.3	Support an individual with dementia to use their abilities during personal care activities	Page 122
3.4	Explain how the attitudes of others may enable an individual with dementia to achieve their potential	Page 122
4.1	Identify some of the anxieties common to carers of an individual with dementia	Page 127

Assessment criteria	What you need to do	Assessment task
DEM 211		
4.2	Outline the legal rights of the carer in relation to an individual with dementia	Page 127
4.3	Involve carers in planning support that enables the rights and choices and protect an individual with dementia from harm	Page 127
4.4	Describe how the need of carers and others to protect an individual from harm may prevent the individual from exercising their rights and choices	Page 127
4.5	Demonstrate how a carer can be supported to enable an individual with dementia to achieve their potential	Page 127

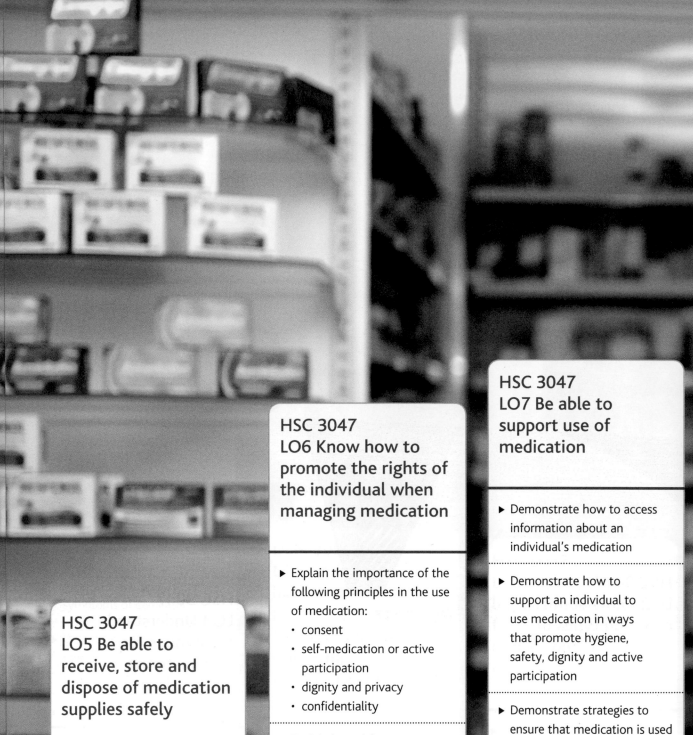

**HSC 3047
LO5 Be able to receive, store and dispose of medication supplies safely**

- ▶ Demonstrate how to receive supplies of medication in line with agreed ways of working

- ▶ Demonstrate how to store medication safely

- ▶ Demonstrate how to dispose of unused or unwanted medication safely

**HSC 3047
LO6 Know how to promote the rights of the individual when managing medication**

- ▶ Explain the importance of the following principles in the use of medication:
  - consent
  - self-medication or active participation
  - dignity and privacy
  - confidentiality

- ▶ Explain how risk assessment can be used to promote an individual's independence in managing medication

- ▶ Describe how ethical issues that may arise over the use of medication can be addressed

**HSC 3047
LO7 Be able to support use of medication**

- ▶ Demonstrate how to access information about an individual's medication

- ▶ Demonstrate how to support an individual to use medication in ways that promote hygiene, safety, dignity and active participation

- ▶ Demonstrate strategies to ensure that medication is used or administered correctly

- ▶ Demonstrate how to address any practical difficulties that may arise when medication is used

- ▶ Demonstrate how and when to access further information or support about the use of medication

CHAPTER 4

HSC 3047
LO8 Be able to record
and report on use of
medication

▶ Demonstrate how to record
use of medication and any
changes in an individual
associated with it

▶ Demonstrate how to report
on use of medication and
problems associated with
medication, in line with
agreed ways of working

Understand the legislative framework for the use of medication in social care settings

Introduction to this chapter

This chapter focuses on the use of medication for individuals with dementia, including people in social care settings. It focuses on knowing and understanding individuals' specific medication needs, broad types, classifications and forms of medication, as well as safe storage, retrieval and disposal of medicines. The chapter covers everything you need to know to complete two closely related optional units of the level 2 Dementia Care Award and Certificate: DEM 305 and HSC 3047.

The term 'legislative framework' refers to the law that governs different aspects of care. Everyone is subject to the law. In health and social care, the law stipulates what care providers should do and what they cannot do. In social care settings, one of the things that the law or the legislative framework governs is the use of medication. The legislative framework dictates what practitioners should do with respect to the use of medication and what they should not do.

There are a number of laws that are aimed at the use and misuse of drugs and medications. The Misuse of Drugs Act (1971) is intended to prevent the non-medical use of certain drugs. These drugs are known as controlled drugs and some can be found in use in social care settings. These include barbiturates, steroids and some tranquilisers. However, the laws that are most likely to affect the use of medication in social care and other settings where individual are living with dementia are:

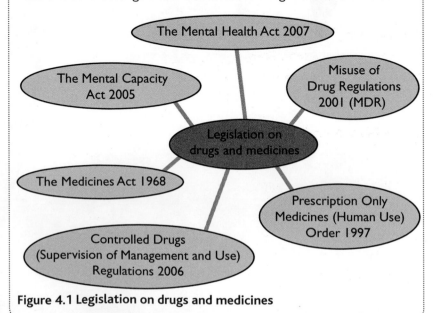

Figure 4.1 Legislation on drugs and medicines

- The Mental Health Act 2007
- The Mental Capacity Act 2005
- Misuse of Drug Regulations 2001 (MDR)
- Legislation on drugs and medicines
- The Medicines Act 1968
- Prescription Only Medicines (Human Use) Order 1997
- Controlled Drugs (Supervision of Management and Use) Regulations 2006

The Medicines Act 1968

This law governs the manufacture and supply of medicine, and affects medications bought at the pharmacist, those prescribed by a doctor and any medicine that is commonly available in many shops and online. It divides medicines into three categories.

1. *Prescription only medicines (POMs)*. These are restricted and cannot be bought in pharmacies or other shops. They can only be sold or supplied by a pharmacist if prescribed by a doctor. An example is a course of antibiotics, which must be prescribed by a doctor. They should only be administered to the individual to whom they are prescribed.

2. *Pharmacy medicines*. These can be sold without a prescription, but only by a pharmacist. An example of a medicine that comes into this category is an inhaler used for hay fever.

3. *General Sales List medicines*. General Sales List medicines can be sold by any shop, not just a pharmacy. Examples are common painkillers such as Paracetamol and Nurofen. However, there are restrictions on the advertising, labelling and production of these medicines. Paracetamol, for instance, can only be bought in limited quantities.

In a social care setting, a worker should not buy medication for any individual in their care. You do not know if it might interact with other medicines the person is taking, or if the individual has an adverse reaction to it.

The Prescription Only Medicines (Human Use) Order 1997

This law lists all the prescription-only medicines (POMs) and who can prescribe them. It provides clarity about the category that any medicine falls in. This is important as it is then possible to differentiate between POMs, pharmacy medicines and General Sales List medicines.

The Controlled Drugs (Supervision of Management and Use) Regulations 2006

The management of controlled drugs falls under the Misuse of Drugs Act (1971). The Controlled Drugs (Supervision of Management and Use) Regulations provide the legislative framework for the control and regulation of controlled drugs. Controlled drugs are medicines that can be prescribed under certain conditions, usually for pain relief.

? Reflect

Think about common medicines you are familiar with. What medicine category do they belong in?

 Investigate

When you next go shopping, examine the general sales medicines that are for sale in shops. What are the most common and what are they remedies for?

The regulations stipulate how the medicines are to be stored so that they cannot be easily accessed by unauthorised people or confused with other categories of drugs (for instance, by being stored in the same place).

The Misuse of Drugs Regulations 2001

The Misuse of Drugs Regulations (2001) govern the use of dangerous and controlled drugs. They make the storage, use and recording of certain medicines extremely important if workers want to avoid the charge of being a drug dealer!

Reflect

Why do you think controlled drugs are governed by additional legislation? To what extent should they be subject to special measures to control their availability?

Investigate

Investigate policies, procedures and agreed ways of working with respect to medication management where you work.

The Mental Health Act 2007

The Mental Health Act (2007) provides for the care and treatment of individuals with mental health problems. Individuals might live in the community or reside in social care settings. In certain circumstances the Act allows doctors to treat individuals for a mental health problem even if the individual does not want to be treated. The treatment is often in the form of medication taken as tablets or as an injection. You should be aware if the individual in your care is subject to a section of the Mental Health Act.

The Mental Capacity Act 2005

This Act aims to protect the interests of individuals who are deemed not to have mental capacity – that is, they are not able to make informed decisions about how they should be cared for. It usually applies to older people with dementia, but other individuals might be subject to the Act. It must be assumed that any individual has the capacity to make their own decisions, unless it is established that the individual lacks capacity. This means the individual should be allowed to decide if they want to take medication, based on sufficient information that allows them to make an informed choice. In a social care setting the individual cannot be compelled to take medication even if the prescriber thinks it is in their best interest to do so, if that individual does not wish to take the medicine.

How and why must practices reflect the legislative requirements?

Policies and procedures and other agreed ways of working must reflect and incorporate the legislative framework because:

- it contributes to the safety of individuals who take medicines as well as other people

- it ensures that the individual has access to the appropriate treatment

- it enables differentiation between different categories of medicines and their use

- it is against the law not to comply with the legislative framework that governs the provision of medicines in social care settings.

Policies and procedures and other agreed ways of working must reflect and incorporate the legislative framework by:

- ensuring the safe and appropriate storage of each category of medicine in line with the legislative framework and regulations

Key term

Mental capacity: the ability to make decisions for yourself

- having suitably trained members of staff to prescribe and administer medicines in the required way

- having measures in place to supervise and check the safe ordering, storage and recording of all prescription-only and other medicines.

Case study – legislation and policies

Amanda, who was completing a placement at a residential home for people with dementia, was asked by a resident's close relative for information about how she could acquire the medicines her mother was given. The relative wanted to take her mother, Mary, who had been in the home for a month, to another home closer to her family.

At first Amanda did not understand what the relative was asking for. The relative did not seem to realise that the medication was prescribed by doctors. The relative said she assumed that the care workers at the home went to the pharmacist in town to buy drugs for the residents. Amanda explained that it was not possible to buy all the medication used and that the use of medication is governed by legislation.

1. Name three pieces of legislation that control the use of medicines.

2. How are medicines classified under the Medicines Act 1968?

3. What could Amanda tell the relative about medicines that are available to buy at the pharmacist?

Knowledge Assessment Task

This assessment task covers HSC 3047 1.1, 1.2, 1.3.

It is important that care workers understand the legislative framework that governs what they do, and this includes laws about the use of medication. In this knowledge assessment task you are required to show that you understand the legislative framework for the use of medication in social care settings.

Imagine you are responsible for training where you work. You are asked to design a training booklet about medication use. The booklet should contain information that:

1. *identifies legislation that governs the use of medication in social care settings*

2. *identifies the legal classification systems for medication*

3. *explains policies and procedures in place in your work area that reflect and incorporate legislative requirements.*

Design the booklet.

 Discuss

Discuss with your line manager how local policies and legislative requirements are complied with in your work setting.

Understand the common medications available to, and appropriate for, individuals with dementia, and their use

To work safely with people living with dementia, practitioners must understand the medications that individuals receive. Workers' awareness should include knowledge about the common types of medications used and why they are prescribed to individuals with dementia. They should be especially aware of the risks and benefits to individuals with dementia who use anti-psychotic medicines. Risks might include adverse changes to a person's mental or physical wellbeing, necessitating accurate recording and reporting of side-effects. As required (PRN) medication is also sometimes necessary, for instance if an individual is in pain.

Common types of medication used to treat individuals with dementia

The most commonly used medications affecting individuals with dementia are:

- medications that manage multi-infarct dementia – dementia resulting from repeated small strokes that lead to damage to the surrounding brain tissue

- medications that help manage subcortical dementias – benign or harmless tumours and hydrocephalus

- medications that offer neuroprotection – that is, protection against further damage – and enhance cognitive ability.

Many older people in health and social care have a cognitive impairment with a type of dementia. While they may have memory problems, they can also experience other symptoms associated with mental health problems such as feeling depressed or having strange and disturbing psychotic experiences. In fact, more people have depression than dementia, and having dementia does not exclude an individual from being depressed as well.

The table on the next page (figure 4.2) outlines a sample of the main types of medicine, names of specific drugs and their use in treating the symptoms of dementia. The generic drug name is given with the UK trade name in brackets.

Your assessment criteria:

DEM 305

1.1 Outline the most common medications used to treat symptoms of dementia.

1.2 Describe how commonly-used medications affect individuals with dementia.

1.3 Explain the risks and benefits of anti-psychotic medication for individuals with dementia.

HSC 3047

2.1 Identify common types of medication.

2.2 List conditions for which each type of medication may be prescribed.

2.3 Describe changes to an individual's physical or mental wellbeing that may indicate an adverse reaction to a medication.

Investigate

Which colleagues in your work setting are able to administer medication? What qualifications do they have?

Key terms

Hydrocephalus: a build-up of fluids in the skull that leads to brain swelling

PRN: an abbreviation of the Latin phrase pro re nata, *meaning in the circumstances or as circumstances arise, used for medicine given as required - instead of on a regular basis*

Figure 4.2 Medication to treat dementia

Type of medicine	Examples of specific drugs	Symptom it is used to treat
Cognitive enhancement and neuroprotection	Donepezil Hydrochloride (Aricept) Galantamine (Reminyl) Rivastigmine (Exelon) Memantine (EBIXA)	Mild to moderate Alzheimer dementia including: short-term memory loss, apathy and lack of motivation Moderate to severe dementia including: loss of memory, poor motivation, confusion and disorientation
Anti-psychotic medication/ neuroleptics	Olanzapine (Zyprexa) Amisulpiride (Solian) Risperidone (Risperdal) Haloperidol (Haldol) Zuclopenthixol (Clopixol) Chlorpromazine (Largactil)	Hearing voices, paranoid ideas delusional and strange beliefs, disrupted thinking
Anti-depressant medication	Doxepine (Sinequan) Citalopram (Cipramil) Fluoxetine (Prozac) Paroxetine (Seroxat) Venlafaxine (Efexor) Mirtazapine (Zispin) Trazodone (Molipaxin) Lofepramine (Gamanil) Amitriptyline (Tryptizol)	Loss of energy and interest, sadness, poor concentration and altered appetite and sleep patterns

What changes to an individual's wellbeing may indicate an adverse reaction to medication?

Individuals can have adverse reactions to any medication, not only those that are used in health and social care settings. The type and severity of effect depends on the medication that is used and the tolerance of the individual to that medicine.

The table opposite illustrates common adverse effects to named medications. While this is not an exhaustive list of medications in each group, they do indicate typical adverse reactions that each category of medicine might cause. It is important that you find out what medication each individual you are looking after is prescribed, and familiarise yourself with the type of adverse effects they may experience.

 Discuss

What adverse reactions to medication have occurred in your care setting? How are they identified through signs and symptoms, and what special actions should be taken in response to them, if any?

Figure 4.3 Common adverse reactions to medications

Type of medicine	Common adverse reactions
Cognitive enhancers including: Donepezil (Aricept), Galantamine (Reminyl) and Rivastigmine (Exelon)	Nausea, vomiting, diarrhoea, insomnia and headache
Anti-psychotics including: Olanzapine (Zyprexa), Amisulpiride (Solian) and Risperidone (Risperdal)	Stiffness, abnormal movements, restlessness, weight gain, apathy and sedation
Anti-depressants including: Doxepine (Sinequan), Citalopram (Cipramil) and Fluoxetine (Prozac)	Sedation, sweating, urinary difficulties, blurred vision, rashes and nausea

Risks and benefits of anti-psychotic medication

Anti-psychotic medication is prescribed for some people with dementia because they experience feelings and thoughts similar to the experiences of people with severe mental health issues. These experiences include thinking that their treasured possessions have been stolen when in reality they have been mislaid or hidden by the individual during a period of confusion. The individual might hear voices, for example believing someone is speaking to them when there is nobody there. Other common symptoms include: strange beliefs, such as that they are being poisoned or thinking the TV or radio is speaking to them personally. These strange ideas can cause distress to the individual and may lead them to behave oddly or out of character. Anti-psychotic medication can reduce or eliminate these distressing symptoms.

However, there are risks to taking anti-psychotic medication. These medications, like all other types of medicine, have side effects. These side effects can raise the risk of misuse of medication – as the side effects include sedation, there is a risk that this kind of medication can be used to quieten down individuals if, for instance, they wander or are noisy or disruptive. The result is over-sedation, a reduction in the quality of life of the individual, which in turn can lead to other physical and psychological problems. Not least among these is similarity between the effects of the misuse of anti-psychotic medication and the symptoms of dementia, in particular apathy and memory problems.

Another side effect to the use of anti-psychotics that puts older people at particular risk is hypotension – a lowering of blood pressure. **Postural hypotension** is a fall in blood pressure when a person stands after lying down or sitting for a long time. This can lead to falls and the older person damaging weakened bone or tissue.

Key term

Postural hypotension: a drop in blood pressure due to a change in body position when a person moves to a more vertical position – from sitting to standing or from lying down to sitting or standing

Rx

Antidepressant

Fluoxetine Hydrochloride

50, 10mg. Tablets

Case study – common types of medication

Parker has Alzheimer's disease, a type of dementia that has affected his memory, leaving him confused about where he is and who other people are. Lately his wife, Angela, rang their doctor and asked him to visit them. She said that Parker had recently hidden the car keys under the mattress and then accused her of taking them so she could give the car to a young man she knew. In fact, the car had been sold months before when Parker was first told he should not drive any more. The keys were spare from another car they had kept from years before and Angela only gave them to Parker because he kept looking for keys.

While Angela was used to Parker's poor memory and confusion, she found it most difficult when he complained about the young people in the next room talking about him. At times he would shout and say he knew that she planned to leave him for the young man she kept inviting into the house.

1. Name two types of medication the doctor might want to prescribe for Parker.

2. What adverse side effects to the medication would you inform Angela and Parker about?

3. How could anti-psychotic medication help Parker?

4. What risks might there be associated with anti-psychotic medication?

Reflect

Individuals with dementia often demonstrate signs of other conditions such as depression or psychosis. Reflect on ways you might identify if an individual is depressed or psychotic in addition to having dementia.

Knowledge Assessment Task

This assessment task covers DEM 305 1.1, 1.2, 1.3 and HSC 3047 2.1, 2.2, 2.3.

An understanding of the use and effects of common types of medication will help you support individuals with dementia and contribute to safe and effective practice. In this knowledge assessment task you are required to show that you know about common types of medication and their use with individuals with dementia.

While working in a social care setting with individuals with dementia you are asked by three families, each of which has a relative you are supporting, to give them information about the medication their relative is using.

What would you tell each family about a common type of medication, the conditions it is prescribed for, and any potential adverse reactions?

Family 1 – the relative has dementia and has psychotic experiences

Family 2 – the relative has dementia and is being treated for depression

Family 3 – the relative has dementia

Record your answers in a way acceptable to your assessor.

Discuss

Discuss with colleagues where you work the risks and benefits of medication. Do colleagues think that it is always better to take medication, or do the risks outweigh any benefit to the individual?

Investigate

All medications have adverse reactions or side effects. Using the BNF (British National Formulary) or BNF online, investigate the side effects to cognitive enhancers such as Aricept, Reminyl and Exelon.

Roles and responsibilities involved in use of medication

While each professional and care worker in social care settings has a duty of care towards individuals they look after, they also have specific roles and responsibilities. These specific roles and responsibilities extend to prescribing, dispensing and supporting the use of medication. Note how care support workers have duties with respect to medication, reflecting their role as working more closely with the individual.

The table below illustrates the key roles and responsibilities of professionals and workers in social care with respect to medication.

Figure 4.4 Roles and responsibilities regarding medication

Title	Role	Key responsibilities
Doctor	To examine the individual and diagnose their health condition or illness To prescribe treatment that might include medication to treat the condition or illness To reassess if the treatment for the condition or illness has been effective To liaise closely with the individual or persons caring for the individual	To ensure that the individual's health status is determined and interventions instigated and monitored
Pharmacist	To confirm that any medication treatment is not going to harm the individual, including the correct dose and means of administration To make the medication available in the correct quantity with instructions for the safe use of the medication To pack the medication in a suitable format, for instance in a dosette box (see overleaf), easy-peel wrapping or other container	To ensure the safe dispensing of medication to the individual or those caring for the individual
Care worker	To communicate with the doctor and pharmacist regarding the medication To ensure the medication is available for the individual as prescribed by the doctor To store the medication safely, complying with local and national guidelines To administer the medication to the individual in the correct dose and by the correct method of administration, or ensure that the individual takes the medication safely as prescribed To observe for adverse reactions and side effects to the medication To dispose of any residual materials safely To record the administration of the medication To monitor the individual's condition or health status	To ensure the safe storage, administration, recording and disposal of medication

While the care worker has specific roles and responsibilities in the administration of medication, as listed on the previous page they also have responsibilities to ensure the individual gives consent to receive medication.

'Over the counter' remedies and supplements

'Over the counter' remedies and supplements are widely available in shops and supermarkets. They can be bought by adults over the age of 18 as remedies for the symptoms of colds or other common ailments, and analgesia for headaches and pains.

Read the case study on the next page, and then answer the questions that follow.

Key term

Dosette box: an individualised box containing medications organised into compartments by day and time, so as to simplify the taking of medications

Reflect

What 'over the counter' medicines do you use? Reflect on why they are easily available and what would be the consequences if they were only available by prescription.

Discuss

Discuss with colleagues their role in respect of medicine management. What do they think is the most important aspect of their role, and why?

Case study

Annie likes to help people. This was one of the reasons she chose a career in social care; there are plenty of opportunities to help and support people in lots of different ways. Mrs Abel (79), whom Annie has got to know quite well from her care work in Meadowside Residential Home, often talks to Annie about what she does when she is not on duty. One day Mrs Abel asks Annie, saying it is because she is so helpful and kind, to get her some vitamin and mineral supplements from a well-known chemist store on the way home. She then offers Annie a £10 note to buy them. Annie feels flattered that Mrs Abel thinks she is helpful and kind; it makes Annie feel good to hear it. She does not like saying 'no' to anyone.

1. What should Annie do?

2. Why should she do this?

Investigate

What policies are in place in your work setting (if any) that concern the relationships between the cared for and the caregivers? Why is it important that people with dementia should be protected from some relationships?

In this case study Annie is put in an awkward position by Mrs Abel. She wants to help her. She should, though, bear in mind the following:

1. Annie does not know what other medication Mrs Abel takes or how the vitamin and mineral supplements would interact with other medication.

2. Has Mrs Abel asked anyone else to do the same errand?

3. What is the policy of Meadowside for residents keeping their own source of medication or other remedies?

4. What is the policy of Meadowside for boundaries of relationships between members of staff and residents?

5. Is it a breach of the guidelines on the administration of medication?

Fortunately Annie realises that she should not buy 'over the counter' remedies or supplements for Mrs Abel – or any other resident. She knows that she would be held responsible should there be any adverse reaction with this older person.

Having reflected on the situation later with her line manager, Annie realises that responsibilities do not just lie with her.

- Meadowside has a responsibility to maintain the safety of all their residents and staff. What would happen if another resident got hold of the supplements and consumed them?

- Meadowside has a responsibility to comply with national and local standards for the safe storage of all medicines including remedies and supplements.

- Meadowside has a responsibility to ensure that care workers are familiar with the policies on medication and its management.

- Annie has a responsibility to maintain the safety of all residents within her capabilities.

- Annie has a responsibility to comply with known national and local policies.

 Reflect

Usually there are many professionals and workers who are involved in the care of an individual with dementia. Of all these people, who has the role and responsibility to ensure that day-to-day medication management is person-centred?

 Investigate

Investigate the policy for medication management where you work. What does it say about using a person-centred approach to medication management?

Discuss

Discuss with your line manager about how the care setting where you work communicates with outside practitioners involved in medication management.

Knowledge Assessment Task

This assessment task covers HSC 3047 3.1, 3.2.

There are many roles carried out by a range of professionals and workers in social care, and care workers should be aware of the responsibilities other practitioners carry. In this knowledge assessment task you are required to show that you understand the roles of others with respect to medication management.

You are asked to depict key roles and responsibilities with respect to medication management as a poster that can be displayed as a reminder for members of staff.

Design a poster that:

1. *describes the roles and responsibilities of those involved in prescribing, dispensing and supporting the use of medication*

2. *explains where responsibilities lie with respect to 'over the counter' remedies and supplements.*

Discuss your ideas for the poster with your assessor before you begin to design it.

Techniques for the administration of medication

Medication comes in different forms and can be administered by a range of means and routes. Special materials and equipment might also be required. As a care worker it is necessary to know about the different routes through which medication can be given, the different forms it may be presented in, and the materials and equipment that might be needed to assist when administering medication.

The routes by which medication can be administered are shown in the table below.

Your assessment checklist:

HSC 3047

4.1 Describe the routes by which medication can be administered.

4.2 Describe different forms in which medication may be presented.

4.3 Describe materials and equipment that can assist in administering medication.

Figure 4.5 Routes to administer medication

Route	Description
Oral or by mouth	This is the most common route for the administration of medication. Tablets, capsules, lozenges and other pills are taken orally, as well as syrups and other medicinal fluids
	Some inhalers are taken orally, such as with asthma
Gastrostomy tube	A gastrostomy tube may be used if it is already in place and the person cannot take anything by mouth
Sublingual or under the tongue	A lozenge is placed under the tongue for quick absorption
Subcutaneous or under the skin	This is by the means of a needle, which is placed under the skin to administer medication in fluid form
Intramuscular or in the muscle	This route involves a needle piercing the skin to administer medication deep into the muscle. This is often given in the gluteus maximus or buttock, or in the upper arm
Anal or rectal	A medication in the form of a suppository is inserted into the rectum
Optical or in the eye	Drops are placed in the eye(s)
Aural or in the ear	Drops are placed in the ear(s)
Topical or on the surface	Creams or lotions are applied to the skin
Nasal or via the nose	Hay fever sprays are an example
Nasogastric tube	A nasogastric tube may be used for some medication if it is in place and the person cannot take anything by mouth

As well as being administered via a range of routes, medication can be presented in different forms:

Figure 4.6 Ways of presenting medication

Some medication can be administered comparatively simply, for instance as a tablet taken from a plastic bottle. However, some medications require special equipment if they are to be administered properly and safely.

Material and equipment to assist in administering medication

The material and equipment used when administering medication depends on the technique and route of administration. A single tablet administered in a health or social care setting requires a small medicine cup to transfer the tablet between the person giving the medicine and the person receiving the medicine. This is to ensure the tablet remains safe and clean. Medication administered by injection, on the other hand, requires specialist equipment to make sure it is administered in an appropriate and safe way.

Materials can refer to an assemblage of items such as antiseptic swabs, gauze and plasters, trays and medicine pots, and dosette boxes that aid the administration of medication, whereas equipment might refer to the tools that are used, such as syringes, needles and ampoules.

Syringes

A **syringe** is a piece of equipment used with a needle to administer parenteral medication by injection. Parenteral means that it does not make use of the digestive or respiratory system as a tablet would. Injections can be given intramuscularly (into the muscle), subcutaneously (below the skin), intravenously (into a vein) and intradermally (into the skin). Of these, the first two are the most likely to be encountered in a social care setting; intramuscular injections are given as inoculations and to relieve psychotic symptoms, for example, and insulin is injected where the individual has diabetes using a subcutaneous injection.

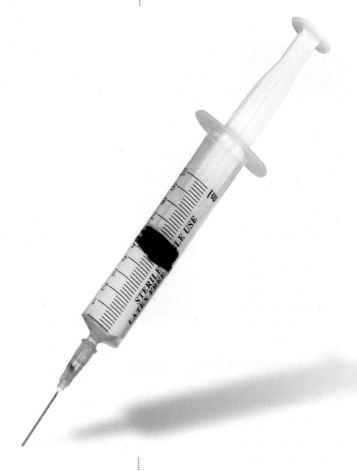

There are several types of syringe, differing in shape and size and made from different materials. Each syringe has three parts: the barrel or outside part, the plunger which fits inside the barrel and the tip where the needle is connected. The types of syringe include:

- hypodermic syringe with a millilitre scale marked on the barrel

- insulin syringe that has a scale specially designed for insulin

- prefilled unit-dose systems that are ready for use or a prefilled cartridge and needles that needs a reusable holder (injection system) to be attached before use.

Needles and ampoules

Needles are made of stainless steel and are usually disposable due to the risk of cross infection if they are shared or used more than once. They are available in different sizes, usually between 1 and 5 centimetres long and #18–#28 in diameter or **gauge**.

Ampoules and vials are used to carry medication that is to be given by injection. An ampoule is a glass container, with a constricted neck varying in size from 1–20 millilitres or more.

🔑 Key terms

Gauge: *needles come in different diameters; a needle gauge is derived from the Birmingham Wire Gauge where the smaller gauge numbers refer to larger needle outer diameters*

Syringe: *a piece of equipment used with a needle to administer an injection*

A vial is a small glass bottle with a sealed rubber cap. A needle is used to pierce the vial through the rubber and then changed for a clean needle to inject the individual.

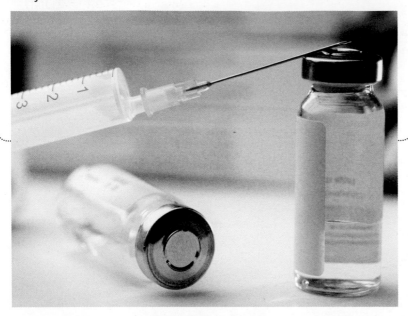

Knowledge Assessment Task

This assessment task covers HSC 3047 4.1, 4.2, 4.3.

Care workers need to understand the techniques used when administering medication as they may be required to assist in medication management. Therefore, it is necessary to know about the different routes through which medication can be given, the different forms it may be presented in, and the materials and equipment that might be needed to assist when administering medication.

In this knowledge assessment task you are required to show that you understand techniques for administering medication.

With the support and permission of your line manager, investigate all the different medications used by individuals in the care setting where you work. For each medication:

1. *identify the route by which it is administered*

2. *identify different forms it can be presented in*

3. *describe materials and equipment that can assist on administering medication*

4. *identify any other forms of medication, routes of administering, materials and equipment that are not used where you work.*

Present your findings in a format acceptable to your assessor.

How to receive, store and dispose of medication supplies safely

When receiving supplies of medication you must always work within policies and ways of working. This is to ensure the security of the medication and everyone's safety.

Read the following case study and then answer the questions that follow.

Your assessment checklist:

HSC 3047

5.1 Demonstrate how to receive supplies of medication in line with agreed ways of working.

5.2 Demonstrate how to store medication safely.

5.3 Demonstrate how to dispose of unused or unwanted medication safely.

Case study

Caroline works at Longside Residential Home for older people with dementia and other long-term conditions, for which they need considerable support in activities of everyday living.

One morning she notices the car from the local pharmacy pull up in the grounds of the home and goes to welcome the driver. About this time every week they receive a supply of the medication required by the residents for the coming week. Caroline is pleased to see that it is Davy Jones delivering the medicines. She likes him and the stories he tells about life on the road as he does his delivery round.

Davy enters carrying a locked container with the medication. Caroline greets him and takes him to the back office – the locked room where medicines, syringes and other medical equipment is stored. On the way she shows a confused resident where the day room is. She asks Davy to put the locked medicines transportation container down on the table and then opens it in front of him, looks briefly inside and offers him a coffee. He accepts so they go to the kitchen.

1. In what ways did Caroline neglect to ensure the security of the medication?

2. In what ways did Caroline put others at risk?

It is vital that care workers are aware of local policies and comply with agreed ways of working. In what ways might Caroline not have complied with agreed ways of working?

- She has not shared the information with the Home's manager that the medication has arrived.

- There is no indication that she or anyone else signed to formally receive the medicines.

- The medicines have not been checked or stored correctly.

- She left the medicine box open and unattended.

- She did not lock the door to the back office.

? Reflect

There will be arrangements for medication to be delivered to your work setting. Reflect on how confidentiality and safety can be compromised if proper procedures are not followed.

 Investigate

How are medicines ordered and delivered where you work? Who orders them and when? What documentation is used?

How to store medicines safely

All medicines must be stored in a way that complies with local policies. These policies will include:

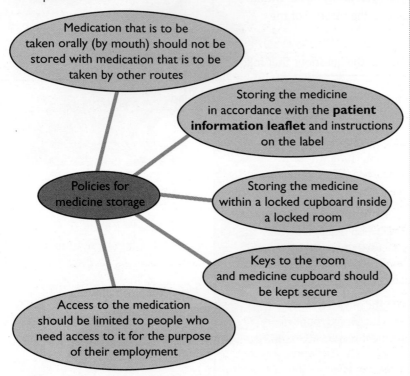

Medication that is to be taken orally (by mouth) should not be stored with medication that is to be taken by other routes

Storing the medicine in accordance with the **patient information leaflet** and instructions on the label

Policies for medicine storage

Storing the medicine within a locked cupboard inside a locked room

Keys to the room and medicine cupboard should be kept secure

Access to the medication should be limited to people who need access to it for the purpose of their employment

Figure 4.7 Policies for medicine storage

Unused or unwanted medication

Sometimes medicines are unused, for instance when the individual has a change of prescription. Medicines might also be unwanted for other reasons, such as that they are out of date or the individual for whom they were supplied has moved on elsewhere. An individual may also remove consent to receive treatment after, for instance, an injection is drawn up ready for administration, but the individual then refuses to accept it.

Key term

Patient information leaflet: a small leaflet supplied with medicines that gives details of the medicine, including its use with specific medical conditions, side effects and dosages

Reflect

Why might an individual with dementia refuse their medication?

Whatever the reason the medicines are unused or unwanted, they must be disposed of carefully and with regard to the law.

Unwanted medicines should be returned to a community pharmacy where they can be consigned as medicinal waste, classified as 'household waste' in line with the Controlled Waste Regulations 1992. This includes waste medicines from a person's home and from a residential home.

If a care home also provides nursing care then the community pharmacy cannot accept unwanted medicines as waste. Instead the home must use a licensed waste management company to dispose of the medicine.

- Unwanted or unused medicines should *never* be given to an individual for whom they were not supplied.

- Unwanted or unused medicines should *never* be removed by staff and used for their own purposes.

- Medicine should never be flushed down a toilet.

- Medicines should never be placed in household refuse bins.

In accordance with agreed ways of working, unwanted or unused medicines should be separated from current medicines at the earliest practical opportunity and transported to the community pharmacy or given to the licensed waste management company for disposal.

Reflect

Are there any particular risks with older people with dementia storing their medication at home? How can any risks be minimised?

Discuss

Discuss with your line manager how medications are stored in your work setting. Which medications can be stored together and which should be stored separately? Do any specific medications require refrigeration or room temperature storage? Why is this?

Investigate

Investigate how medications where you work are disposed of. Is a licenced waste company used or are they sent to the community pharmacist? What procedures are followed?

Practical Assessment Task

This assessment task covers HSC 3047 5.1, 5.2, 5.3.

Care workers need to be able to practise safely with respect to medication. This is particularly necessary where individuals have dementia because there are risks present that are different from risks in other client groups. Safe medication management begins with workers being able to receive, store and dispose of medication supplies safely.

For this practical assessment task you are required to demonstrate that you are able to receive, store and dispose of medication supplies safely.

1. *Discuss agreed ways of working on receiving, storing and disposing of medication with your line manager.*

2. *Investigate policies and procedures in your work setting about medication management.*

3. *Demonstrate to your assessor's satisfaction that you can receive, store and dispose of medication safely.*

4. *Provide evidence that you can receive, store and dispose of medication safely as a 300 word written account that includes specific governing legislation.*

Promoting individuals' rights when managing medication

As in other areas of life, individuals have rights in relation to taking medication, and care workers have a duty in upholding these rights. This is particularly so when individuals are vulnerable – for example, when they have dementia. There are actions care workers can carry out that support and promote the rights of individuals while managing medication, and they are important for the reasons explained in the table below.

Using risk assessments to promote independence during medication management

Risk assessments on the use of medication are carried out to assess potential and actual risks to individuals concerning medication. The suitability of the medicine is assessed, but so are the means and circumstances in which the medicine is taken. The risk assessment plays an important role in promoting the individual's independence in managing medication.

Read the four vignettes on pages 157–8. They demonstrate different ways that risk assessment promotes the individual's independence in managing medication.

Your assessment checklist:

HSC 3047

6.1 Explain the importance of the following principles in the use of medication:
- consent
- self-medication or active participation
- dignity and privacy
- confidentiality.

6.2 Explain how risk assessment can be used to promote an individual's independence in managing medication.

6.3 Describe how ethical issues that may arise over the use of medication can be addressed.

Figure 4.8 Supporting rights when managing medication

Right	Explanation
The right to consent to treatment	That the individual gives permission to be treated is a legal requirement. The process of establishing consent is also one way that care workers can demonstrate that they respect the individual, and is instrumental in developing trust between the care worker and the person being cared for.
The right to actively participate in treatment	Enabling the individual, when it is possible, to actively participate in their treatment through self-medication is important because it helps promote the individual's autonomy and control over their care and treatment.
The right to dignity, privacy and respect	The individual retains their dignity and privacy. This is particularly important when receiving medication that involves a procedure, such as an injection, where clothing is arranged. Privacy is not only one way that care workers can show that they respect the individual, but is also a fundamental human right. The right to privacy is encoded by the articles of the Human Rights Act (1998).
The right to confidentiality	Maintaining confidentiality ensures that the individual's privacy and dignity are not undermined by information about them being shared and discussed by others who have no need to know what medication an individual receives.

Vignette 1

Clarice is 93 years old. She has vascular dementia, but still lives alone in a warden-controlled flat. Twice a day she is supported with taking her medicine. Although she is quite frail, and has rheumatism, the care worker only has to take Clarice's tablets from the packet. Clarice likes a glass of water to help the tablets go down, which she insists on getting herself. However, there are risks involved.

The risk assessment identified walking with a glass of water from the kitchen as a risk, but it is positive risk-taking. It respected Clarice's preferences and promoted her independence with her medication management.

Vignette 2

Sandar is 63 and has an early-onset type of dementia. She does not think there is anything wrong with her, even though she has been behaving oddly – putting the kettle in the oven to boil water and trying to light the electric radiators with a match. She is being assessed for residential care by her social worker. Her husband explains that when it is time for her to have her medicine, a cognitive enhancer called Reminyl, she often refuses. He spends a great deal of time explaining to Sandar what the medicine is for, and why she should take it, before she consents to taking the Reminyl. The social worker notes that there are actual risks to Sandar from her behaviour, and potential risks to her. The risk assessment questions if she being coerced into taking her medication, or whether she needs it for her own good.

Because Sandar had presented risks with her behaviour, the risk assessment elements that focused on her medicine management advocated that she should be persuaded to take medicine even if at first she refused. Ultimately this would maintain her level of independence, as otherwise she may have had to be taken into residential care for her own safety.

Vignette 3

Morgan lives in Milkwood, a specialist residential home for older people with dementia. The staff take care of all his everyday needs. His independence in medicine management is promoted after each meal. He likes to help the care staff by clearing some of the tables away before accepting his tablets, but is then reminded and encouraged to collect his medicine from the trolley instead of it being brought to him. In view, though, of his contentment with this arrangement, and his other 'jobs' at the facility, it was decided in consultation with Morgan, and his son, that he should continue clearing the tables away before accepting his tablets.

 Investigate

In what ways does risk assessment where you work contribute to an individual's independence, and how might risk assessment be a barrier to independence?

His independence is promoted as he chooses to take the medication when he is ready.

Vignette 4

Rodney has recently been diagnosed with Alzheimer's disease. It is in the early stages and he can continue to live much as he did before his memory started to deteriorate. As a single man, he thought he might have to rely on friends and neighbours for support with his medication. However, it was decided after a risk assessment was carried out that his independence could be promoted and supported if he did as much of the medication management himself for as long as he is able. He collects his prescription from the local chemist who conveniently supplies his cognitive enhancer in weekly packs. This arrangement works well. He is able to self-medicate, checked weekly by the pharmacist.

Each of these vignettes illustrates a way that risk assessments can promote the individual's independence. They should, however, be carried out by a trained worker and in consultation as far as possible with the individual and those who know him or her well.

Ethical issues

Ethics concerns what people do and why they take certain actions. It is a code for behaviour and a branch of moral philosophy that tries to differentiate between what is right and what is wrong.

In social care, and particularly with individuals with dementia, there are a number of ethical issues that affect medication management. Individuals with dementia are vulnerable and often their family carers are vulnerable as well. Therefore great care should be taken to think about the ethics, or what is right and what is wrong, regarding each situation. For instance, dementia can bring with it ethical dilemmas concerning what is the right course of action. Sometimes, what seems the right thing to do in a certain situation may also have harmful effects, and so might be the wrong action.

Typical ethical dilemmas encountered with people with dementia include issues around consent, individual autonomy, confidentiality, iatrogenic adverse effects, beneficence and maleficence and the duty to avoid harm to people you care for.

The table opposite explains some of the ethical issues, and how they might be addressed.

Key terms

Beneficence: *an ethical term meaning that action is taken for the good of others*

Iatrogenesis: *an inadvertent ill effect or adverse reaction to medical treatment*

Maleficence: *the intention to harm others. Non-maleficence is an ethical term that means the intention to avoid doing harm*

Discuss

Ask a colleague to discuss ethical issues they have experienced with individuals with dementia. What was the issue and who was involved? Was there a resolution to the issue and, If so, how was it resolved?

Discuss

Talk with your line manager about the ethical dilemmas they have encountered in the care setting. How were they addressed?

Figure 4.9 Ethical issues surrounding medication of individuals with dementia

Ethical issue	Explanation	Ways it can be addressed
Informed consent	The individual with dementia may not understand why they are offered medicine and as such do not give informed consent for treatment	Frequent explanations of why the medication is prescribed Discussion with family, and other carers, about the individual's preferences with respect to taking medication
Confidentiality	Confidentiality can be breached as others, not just the individual older person, may need to be involved in decisions about medication management	To seek the individual's permission to discuss issues with family and others who know them well
Autonomy	The autonomy or independence of the individual is affected, perhaps by a new reliance on medication	The individual should be encouraged and enabled to participate actively in their own medication management as far as they are able. This includes, if possible, where to have medication, when and in what form
Iatrogenesis	Iatrogenic effects – unintended adverse reactions to medication – can include complex drug reactions as older people are often prescribed more than one medication for a number of health conditions	Medication should be monitored closely and reviewed on a regular basis
Beneficence and maleficence	Care workers have a duty to do good (beneficence) and avoid harming (maleficence) the people they care for. Physiological changes during older age can lead to specific problems including cumulative effects and toxicity from impaired circulation, slower absorption of medication substances and decreased muscle mass (affecting intramuscular injections)	The physical health and condition of the older person should be monitored closely and reviewed on a regular basis Assessments of injection sites should be made. Shorter needles may be needed for injections

 Reflect

Individuals with dementia have rights like everybody else. In what ways do you think care workers have to work hard in protecting these individuals' rights with respect to the management of medication?

Discuss

Ask your line manager or supervisor to discuss how self-medication could be promoted where you work. What are the potential challenges and how might they be overcome, if at all?

Knowledge Assessment Task

This assessment task covers HSC 3047 6.1, 6.2, 6.3.

Individuals with dementia have rights, including those relating to medication. To uphold these rights, the suitability of any medication given to individuals with dementia should be assessed as well as the means and circumstances in which the medicine is taken. Risk assessment plays an important role in promoting the individual's independence in managing medication. In this knowledge assessment task you are required to show that you know how to promote the rights of individuals when managing their medication the following.

In a format acceptable to your assessor, and providing examples from your care setting, explain the following:

1. *the importance of:*

   - *establishing consent*

   - *self-medication or active participation*

   - *dignity and privacy*

   - *confidentiality*

2. *how risk assessments can be used in promoting three individuals' independence in managing medication*

3. *how ethical issues may arise over the use of medication for individuals with dementia, giving three examples from your care setting.*

 Investigate

Using the internet, investigate how medication can affect individuals' dignity and privacy. What happens if individual do not consent to having medication? Is their dignity respected if everybody else thinks they should have it?

How can care workers support the use of medication?

Care workers have a key role in supporting the use of medication. In doing so they should be able to access information about an individual's medication, and demonstrate how to support an individual's use of medication in ways that promote hygiene, safety, dignity and active participation. They need to show that they can ensure medication is used or administered correctly, and also know how and when to access further information or support about the use of medication.

The safe management of medication must comply with relevant legislation and conform to local policies and agreed ways of working in the particular care setting. Following these standards and guidelines should ensure that the process of administering is safe and respectful of individuals.

Can adhering to instructions be person-centred?

It is a requirement, and good practice expected of all workers in health and social care settings, that they provide person-centred care to individuals with dementia. This includes using a person-centred approach to the appropriate and effective use of medication. Person-centredness is a way of working that aims to put the individual at the centre of the care situation, taking into account their personality, wishes and preferences.

This can be accomplished in a range of different ways, some of which are described in the case study about Milkwood on pages 164–5. A person-centred approach might include the following:

- understanding the normal routine of the individual, and accommodating the administering of medication around it

- as far as possible, meeting the preferences and wishes of the individual, for example prescribing liquids instead of tablets, having medication at a certain time (depending on the type and use of the medication) and in a preferred place (some people would rather take their medication in their room, for instance)

- helping the individual take their medication, for example giving one tablet at a time and starting with the smallest

- enabling the individual to self-administer their own medication. In social care settings this might need careful observation, and it should not be excluded or enabled without a proper risk assessment.

At all times, even when using a person-centred approach to medication management in dementia, administration instructions should be followed.

Your assessment checklist:

DEM 305

1.5 Describe how 'as required' (PRN) medication can be used to support individuals with dementia who may be in pain

2.1 Describe person-centred ways of administering medicines while adhering to administration instructions

? **Reflect**

Reflect on how you could get to know the normal routine of an individual with dementia. What might the challenges be?

Is all medication prescribed as a regular and consistent dose?

In some circumstances the person who is administering medication to clients or service users has some discretion about what to give. This is known as PRN medication, sometimes called 'as required' medication, because it is administered as required by the individual, but at the discretion of the person with the responsibility for giving it.

PRN stands for *pro re nata*, a Latin phrase meaning 'in the circumstances' or 'as circumstances arise'. There are a number of uses that can be made of PRN medication in dementia: to help an individual sleep at night, for instance if they are disorientated and think it is daytime; or to calm the individual if they are in extreme psychological distress following the experience of hearing voices of people who are not there.

 Discuss

Discuss with a colleague the ways that individuals with dementia can be helped with taking medication. How can individuals' preferences be taken account of?

PRN medication should never be given regularly. It is for certain circumstances only. Should it appear to be needed regularly then the circumstances should be discussed with the care team, including the doctor responsible for treatment, and the care plan and prescribed medication reviewed.

However, a common use of PRN medication in dementia is for individuals who are in pain. Many older people experience pain: in their joints from arthritis or rheumatism, from skin complaints or headaches associated with eyesight problems and poor vision. Other causes of pain in older people include: poor diet and dehydration, adverse reactions to medication, and fractures.

Sometimes, individuals with dementia are not able to express themselves clearly. The care worker should therefore be vigilant for individuals in pain and take the appropriate action. This might be to:

- observe for grimacing or another indication the individual is in pain

- listen for groaning or moaning

- ask the individual if they are in pain

- be aware of changes in the way an individual walks or sits

- know about the individual's personal history, and in particular their medical history.

PRN medication for pain relief can then be offered, and any effects monitored to determine whether the pain ceases or continues. Remember that if you suspect pain you should alert and discuss it with other members of the care team and make sure the individual's care and prescription is assessed.

? Reflect

Reflect on how you communicate that you are in pain. Compare it with a person with dementia who has problems communicating.

The organisation of care

The organisation of care is extremely important. Disorganised care is poor care; it is not safe and is unlikely to be effective. Medication management must be organised. The organisation of care is discussed next: accessing information about medication, supporting individuals to use medication correctly; responding to practical difficulties that might arise and looking at when and how to seek further assistance and information.

Read the following case study about Milkwood, a residential care home for older people with dementia. Isabelle, a registered nurse, is in charge; and Wandy is newly arrived from southern Africa for her first job in a UK social care setting. She is about to experience supporting the use of medication in a residential care setting for the first time.

When you have finished reading about Milkwood, answer the questions that follow.

Case study – Milkwood, 1: Monday

Milkwood has 30 residents, and one more is expected to be admitted later on today for assessment. The home is usually staffed by four care workers during day shifts and two at night. There is always a registered nurse on duty to lead the care team and be responsible for the daily management of Milkwood. Today Isabelle, the registered nurse, is on duty.

One of the care workers is Wandy. She is from southern Africa, and has been living in Britain for just over a month. Today she is working with two other care workers, Sophie and Benjamin.

There is a fixed routine at the home to provide structure to the day, to help residents remember what is happening and to ensure that activities including recreational and occupational activities are carried out. The morning routine begins with supporting people to get up, wash or shower, and dress before breakfast. This is soon followed by the 'medicine round', where medication is administered to residents as per their prescription chart.

After breakfast, Isabelle asks Wandy to assist her in administering medication. They both wash their hands. A trolley containing the medication is brought out to the spacious hallway where Isabelle unlocks it and sets out all the prescription cards. She asks Wandy to fetch some fresh water in a plastic jug and then starts to study the prescription charts for residents who are to have medicines.

She notes that Clarice, a 93-year-old resident, newly admitted for respite with vascular dementia, is prescribed soluble aspirin. Isabelle waits for the tablet to dissolve before taking it to Clarice while Wandy watches the trolley. Clarice says that she likes to put the aspirin in the water herself and asks if there is any reason why she shouldn't. Isabelle, who cannot think of any reason why Clarice cannot put the aspirin in to dissolve, so long as there is someone to watch her, wants to discuss it first with the care team. She also wants to conduct a risk assessment so any issues can be identified.

Bernie, one of the residents who has Alzheimer's disease, needs support to take his tablets. He finds it difficult to swallow. Isabelle notes that the tablet is 'scored', having a dividing line along its diameter. This is so that the tablet can be snapped in half. This she does, to make the two halves more manageable for Bernie. She also thinks that it would be better if he could have a liquid medicine instead, and plans to look in the BNF (British Nationals Formulary, a compendium of medicines commonly used in hospitals and other care settings to ensure medicines are used correctly and safely), to see if a liquid alternative to the tablet is available. She could then talk about the possible change with Bernie. First she discusses it with Wandy to assess whether it has been a problem for Bernie at other times.

The medicine round goes as planned as the last prescription card is opened. It is for Morgan, whom Isabelle sees clearing tables. She notes that he has a cognitive enhancer, but wants to check the dose to ensure it is correct. She looks in the BNF to check as she waits for Morgan to finish clearing the tables. He then ambles to the trolley to collect his medication.

After the medicine round Isabelle talks with Wandy about Bernie's difficulty swallowing tablets. They decide to bring it up later that day at handover.

Now answer these questions.

1. How did Isabelle access information about individuals' medication?

2. In what ways did Isabelle support an individual to use medication hygienically, correctly and safely?

3. How was active participation by individuals promoted?

In the Milkwood case study, the medication round goes to plan with no hitches or unexpected difficulties. However, this is not always the case.

Discuss

Discuss with your line manager or supervisor how medications are organised and ask to participate in medication management.

Does medication management always go to plan?

By following national and local standards and agreed ways of working, the management of medication should be safe and respectful of individuals. However, sometimes during medication management there might be some practical difficulties that arise due to organisational issues. These include:

- late delivery of medicines or delivery during busy periods such as handover times or during meals

- administering medication to a large number of clients at the same time, for example before or after a meal

- the layout of a residential facility that makes it difficult to find individuals for their medication

- distractions such as the phone ringing or an individual seeking assistance.

These are only a sample of potential practical organisational difficulties that might occur during medication management. Now read more about Milkwood.

Case study – Milkwood, 2: Tuesday

Wandy is a care worker at Milkwood Residential Home for people with dementia. She is helping Isabelle, the registered nurse, to administer medication to the residents. It is now just past 1 p.m. and the residents are finishing their mid-day meal. Benjamin and Sophie are in the bathroom making sure it is clean and safe for residents' use later.

Isabelle tells her that Bernie's new medication, which has now been prescribed in liquid form because it is easier for him to swallow, has not been delivered. She asks Wandy to check the stock room for the medication box to see if it had arrived when she was unavailable. Wandy does so and returns to say it is not there.

Meanwhile Morgan has come to the trolley for his tablet, but he is not prescribed one until the evening. As Isabelle explains this to him, there is a phone call from the community chemist, wanting to speak to the person in charge. Wandy watches the trolley, which Isabelle locks, before going to the phone to ask about Bernie's medicine. It appears that the medicine is on its way but will be about another half an hour.

1. What potential practical difficulties have arisen?

2. What might Isabelle do to avoid these difficulties occurring again?

It is not easy to predict every practical difficulty that might arise in a social care setting, especially one where individuals have dementia. The individuals are vulnerable and need to be protected; abiding with standards and guidance is one way of ensuring their safety. Good day-to-day management is another way.

Isabelle might have carried out the following to ensure that potential practical difficulties were minimised:

- checked for the delivery of Bernie's new medication before she began the medicine round

- asked Wandy to tell the chemist that she would phone them back as soon as she had completed the medicine round

- arranged with the chemist and other regular callers not to phone at certain times in the future

- had all care staff on duty available at meal and medicine times.

What other practical issues might arise?

In addition to practical difficulties that arise due to organisational reasons, there are difficulties that stem from the medications themselves and failings in their management, whether the failings are due to the individual or the person responsible for administering the medication.

The table on the next page (figure 4.10) outlines a range of practical difficulties that might arise, and actions that can be taken in response to the difficulties.

Investigate

Investigate the care environment where you work. To what extent does it help or hinder the organisation of medication management?

Discuss

Discuss with colleagues what else happens when medication is administered. How far is medication administration prioritised in the daily routine of the care setting?

Figure 4.10 Practical issues surrounding medication management

Practical difficulty	What should be done
Medication might be lost, missing or damaged accidentally	In these situations the person responsible should be informed and the medication replaced as soon as practicable
An individual decides that they do not want to take medication that is prescribed for them	The purpose of the medication and potential ill-effects should be explained to the individual to establish informed consent. If the individual still does not want the medication, the prescriber and person in charge at the care setting should be informed
Difficulty in taking the medication	Some individuals with dementia lose the swallowing reflex and cannot take medication easily. Their medication might be available in alternative forms, for example as a liquid instead of tablets. The prescriber should be informed
The wrong medication is used	In these situations the individual should be observed and monitored for adverse effects, emergency action taken if necessary (consult the medication information sheet, a pharmacist or doctor or NHS Direct), and the prescriber informed
Vomiting after taking medication	The individual should be observed and monitored for a recurrence of the vomiting and any other signs of illness. The medication should not be administered again without consultation with the prescriber
Adverse reactions	These should be recorded and the individual monitored and assessed for their health status. The prescriber should be consulted
Discrepancies in records or directions for use	If there is any discrepancy in the records about what the individual should have, the medication should not be given until the correct record is established. The medication should not be given until medication, dose, time, technique and route of administration is confirmed with the prescriber

At Milkwood, Isabelle and Wandy acted as advocates for Bernie because he had difficulty swallowing tablets. It is important in social care settings that care workers act as advocates for individuals in their care who may be prescribed medication. It is even more important that they advocate for individuals with dementia because individuals might:

- be vulnerable to abuse and exploitation

- be experiencing difficulties in communication and expressing themselves

- be marginalised and not listened to

- be experiencing adverse effects or reactions that they are not aware of

- not understand the care system

- not know that options or alternative treatments might be available to them.

 Discuss

Discuss advocacy with colleagues. In what ways are they advocates for individuals in their care? What issues do they advocate on, and with whom?

What support and further information is available?

Being able to support the use of medication is an activity that is shared between different care workers and professionals, even if there is only one person who actually administers the medicine. Sometimes it is necessary to seek further information or support about the use of medication. How and when should care workers access further information or support about the use of medication? Support or further information should be sought in the following circumstances:

- *The person working with medications is not familiar with a certain medicine.* The worker should find out about any medicine that they administer. They can get more information about medication in the BNF and the medication's information leaflet. This is important. Unless the effects of and adverse reactions to a medication are understood, the caregiver will not know if it is working or if the individual is experiencing adverse effects to the medication.

- *There is a practical difficulty.* Practical difficulties can arise unexpectedly despite care workers following policies and procedures closely. Support should be sought in the first instance from the line manager or person in charge in the care setting. It is important to remember that the purpose of seeking support is not to apportion blame, but to ensure the safety of individuals and others. (Practical difficulties are discussed on pages 167–8.)

Investigate

Investigate internet sources of information about medicines. Which websites contain information that is easiest to understand? Why do you think the information they supply can be relied on, or not relied on?

Knowledge Assessment Task

This assessment task covers DEM 305 1.5, 2.1, 2.2.

Medication management using a person-centred approach means taking into account the wishes and preferences of the individual while complying with instructions for use of medication. For this knowledge assessment task you are required to show that you understand the appropriate use of PRN medication, person-centred ways of administering medication, and advocating for individuals with respect to their medication.

With the permission of your line manager:

1. *identify PRN medication that is prescribed in your care setting and discuss why, when and how it is used*

2. *collate this information in a format that is acceptable to your assessor*

3. *discuss your findings with your assessor*

4. *write a letter to your assessor and, in 200 words, explain the importance of advocating for one individual in your care.*

Practical Assessment Task

This assessment task covers HSC 3047 7.1, 7.2, 7.3, 7.4, 7.5.

Being able to support the use of medication is a skill that is highly valued when carried out safely and using a person-centred approach. This practical assessment task requires you to demonstrate your ability to support the use of medication, including when and how to seek further information and assistance.

With the support of your line manager and the consent of an individual in your care:

1. *access medication information about two individuals*

2. *support them in the use of medication in ways that promote hygiene, safety, dignity and active participation*

3. *support them in ways to use medication correctly*

4. *reflect on three practical difficulties that might arise, and outline to your assessor how you would address these difficulties*

5. *identify two situations when you might need to access further information and two situations when you might need to seek assistance when supporting the use of medication.*

 Reflect

Reflect on the different ways that a person-centred approach to medication management is affected by dementia. Why is a person-centred approach the best option for the individual?

 Discuss

Discuss with your line manager how you ensure that medication is used correctly and is administered in line with the individual's wishes and preferences. Try to discuss specific examples.

Investigate

Investigate ways to promote hygiene when administering medication. Do different techniques require different approaches to hygiene? Do they need any special measures?

Recording and reporting the use of medication

It is a requirement that workers record and report on the use of medication, including the presence of side effects and adverse reactions to medication, remembering that often individuals with dementia may not be able to report problems themselves. The use of medication and any changes to an individual associated with its use, or any other problem such as a practical difficulty, should be recorded in line with agreed ways of working.

How and when a record should be made of the use of medication

Records of the use of medication should be made on the local record of administration card in line with agreed policies and ways of working:

- The record should be clear, accurate and immediate – not written sometime after the event. The record should be signed and dated, with the signature legible, so that it can be checked who administered the medicine.

- A record should be made on the record of administration card if the medication is intentionally withheld from the individual; this might be because the individual was unwell at the time, or an adverse reaction had been noted.

- A record should be made on the record of administration card if the medication is refused by the individual.

- A record should be made on the record of administration card if the individual is absent at the time, for example, when on an outing with family.

Your assessment checklist:

DEM 305

1.4 Explain the importance of recording and reporting side effects/adverse reactions to medication.

HSC 3047

8.1 Demonstrate how to record use of medication and any changes in an individual associated with it.

8.2 Demonstrate how to report on use of medication and problems associated with medication, in line with agreed ways of working.

 Discuss

Discuss with your line manager or supervisor who you should report to on the use of medication. What are the agreed ways of working when reporting on medication use?

171

Knowledge Assessment Task

This assessment task covers DEM 305 1.4.

Safe medication management demands proper and accurate recording and reporting. In order to understand the use of medication it is also necessary to understand any adverse reactions individuals might experience from taking medication. Any reactions must be recorded and reported to those responsible for the prescribing and management of medication. In this knowledge assessment task you are required to explain the importance of recording and reporting side effects/adverse reactions to medication.

1. *Make a list of each medication used in your care setting, and for each identify the side effects and adverse reactions using the BNF or the BNF online.*

2. *Which side effects/adverse reactions are most common for each type of medication?*

Practical Assessment Task

This assessment task covers HSC 3047 8.1, 8.2.

With the support of your line manager and the consent of individuals in your care, this practical assessment task requires you to:

1. *participate in the administering of medication to individuals*

2. *record the use of medication and any changes in an individual associated with it*

3. *report to your line manager any side effects or adverse reactions you identified*

4. *write a 200-word account about how you recorded the use of medication, who you reported to and what you reported.*

? | Reflect

The use of medication should always be recorded. Reflect on the potential consequences if the use of medication is not recorded.

Discuss

How are adverse reactions to medication reported? Discuss with your line manager any procedures that are in use where you work.

Investigate

Investigate how the administering of medication is recorded where you work. Are prescription administration cards used? Is reporting documented anywhere else?

Assessment checklist

The assessment of this unit is partly knowledge-based (assessing things you need to know about) and partly competence-based (assessing things you need to do in the real work environment). To complete this unit successfully, you will need to produce evidence of both your knowledge and your competence.

The knowledge-based assessment criteria for DEM 305 and HSC 3047are listed in the 'What you need to know' table below. The practical or competence-based criteria for HSC 3047 are listed in the 'What you need to do' table opposite. Your tutor or assessor will help you to prepare for your assessment, and the tasks suggested in the chapter will help you to create the evidence you need.

Assessment criteria	What you need to know	Assessment task
DEM 305		
1.1	Outline the most common medications used to treat symptoms of dementia	Page 144
1.2	Describe how commonly-used medications affect individuals with dementia	Page 144
1.3	Explain the risks and benefits of anti-psychotic medication for individuals with dementia	Page 144
1.4	Explain the importance of recording and reporting side effects/adverse reactions to medication	Page 172
1.5	Describe how 'as required' (PRN) medication can be used to support individuals with dementia who may be in pain	Page 170
2.1	Describe person-centred ways of administering medicines while adhering to administration instructions	Page 170
2.2	Explain the importance of advocating for an individual with dementia who may be prescribed medication	Page 170

Assessment criteria	What you need to know	Assessment task
HSC 3047		
1.1	Identify legislation that governs the use of medication in social care settings	Page 140
1.2	Outline the legal classification system for medication	Page 140
1.3	Explain how and why policies and procedures or agreed ways of working must reflect and incorporate legislative requirements	Page 140
2.1	Identify common types of medication	Page 144
2.2	List conditions for which each type of medication may be prescribed	Page 144
2.3	Describe changes to an individual's physical or mental wellbeing that may indicate an adverse reaction to a medication	Page 144
3.1	Describe the roles and responsibilities of those involved in prescribing, dispensing and supporting use of medication	Page 148
3.2	Explain where responsibilities lie in relation to use of 'over the counter' remedies and supplements	Page 148
4.1	Describe the routes by which medication can be administered	Page 152
4.2	Describe different forms in which medication may be presented	Page 152
4.3	Describe materials and equipment that can assist in administering medication	Page 152
6.1	Explain the importance of the following principles in the use of medication: • consent • self-medication or active participation • dignity and privacy • confidentiality	Page 160
6.2	Explain how risk assessment can be used to promote an individual's independence in managing medication	Page 160
6.3	Describe how ethical issues that may arise over the use of medication can be addressed	Page 160

Assessment criteria	What you need to do	Assessment task
HSC 3047		
5.1	Demonstrate how to receive supplies of medication in line with agreed ways of working	Page 155
5.2	Demonstrate how to store medication safely	Page 155
5.3	Demonstrate how to dispose of unused or unwanted medication safely	Page 155
7.1	Demonstrate how to access information about an individual's medication	Page 170
7.2	Demonstrate how to support an individual to use medication in ways that promote hygiene, safety, dignity and active participation	Page 170
7.3	Demonstrate strategies to ensure that medication is used or administered correctly	Page 170
7.4	Demonstrate how to address any practical difficulties that may arise when medication is used	Page 170
7.5	Demonstrate how and when to access further information or support about the use of medication	Page 170
8.1	Demonstrate how to record use of medication and any changes in an individual associated with it	Page 172
8.2	Demonstrate how to report on use of medication and problems associated with medication, in line with agreed ways of working	Page 172

5 | The nutritional requirements of individuals with dementia

DEM 302
LO1 Understand the nutritional needs that are unique to individuals with dementia

- Describe how cognitive, functional and emotional changes associated with dementia can affect eating, drinking and nutrition

- Explain how poor nutrition can contribute to an individual's experience of dementia

- Outline how other health and emotional conditions may affect the nutritional needs of an individual with dementia

- Explain the importance of recognising and meeting an individual's personal and cultural preferences for food and drink

- Explain why it is important to include a variety of food and drink in the diet of an individual with dementia

DEM 302
LO2 Understand the effect that mealtime environments can have on an individual with dementia

- Describe how mealtime cultures and environments can be a barrier to meeting the nutritional needs of an individual with dementia

- Describe how mealtime environments and food presentation can be designed to help an individual to eat and drink

- Describe how a person-centred approach can support an individual, with dementia at different levels of ability, to eat and drink

CHAPTER 5

**DEM 302
LO3 Be able to support an individual with dementia to enjoy good nutrition**

▶ Demonstrate how the knowledge of life history of an individual with dementia has been used to provide a diet that meets his/her preferences

▶ Demonstrate how meal times for an individual with dementia are planned to support his/her ability to eat and drink

▶ Demonstrate how the specific eating and drinking abilities and needs of an individual with dementia have been addressed

▶ Demonstrate how a person-centred approach to meeting nutritional requirements has improved the wellbeing of an individual with dementia

Nutritional needs unique to individuals with dementia

Introduction to this chapter

This chapter covers the learning and assessment requirements of DEM 302 *Understand and meet the nutritional requirements of individuals with dementia*. The chapter focuses on the ways in which dementia can affect the nutritional status of individuals, as well as the impact of nutrition on a person's experience of dementia. It will help you understand the need to create environments that encourage healthy eating and drinking and guide you in using a range of person-centred skills to enable individuals with dementia to eat and drink well.

Your assessment criteria:

DEM 302

1.1 Describe how cognitive, functional and emotional changes associated with dementia can affect eating, drinking and nutrition.

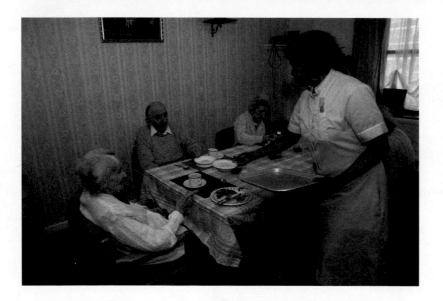

Key terms

Cognitive: mental processes to do with thinking, awareness, knowledge, perception, reasoning and judgment

Delusional ideas: fixed beliefs or perceptions that persist despite evidence to the contrary

Functional: able to fulfil everyday functions and carry out usual behaviours

Nutritional status: physical health in relation to the consumption of nutrients

Paranoia: an unfounded or exaggerated negative state of distrust towards objects and/or people, which can form part of a delusion

In what ways can dementia affect nutrition?

Dementia does not cause weight loss, but it does affect the way a person thinks, behaves and feels, so that everyday activities such as eating and drinking can be detrimentally affected. Over time, this can impact on a person's **nutritional status** and his or her health and wellbeing. As a health and social care worker it is vital to recognise the challenges a person with dementia faces in eating a healthy and balanced diet, because of the impact of:

- cognitive changes

- functional changes

- emotional changes.

Reflect

Think about your diet, the foods you eat and what you drink. Consider how day-to-day changes, such as feeling upset, having a cold, or being anxious, impact on your eating patterns. Try to relate this to the fluctuations in appetite that a person with dementia might experience.

Look at the table in Figure 5.1, which shows the main changes associated with dementia that impact on nutrition. Remember that not all individuals with dementia will experience all of these changes, but it is likely that most will experience some.

 Discuss

Talk with colleagues about your experiences with individuals whose cognitive, functional and emotional deficits from dementia impact on their nutrition. Share strategies for managing these difficulties.

Figure 5.1 How dementia impacts on nutrition

Impacts of dementia on nutrition		
Cognitive changes	**Functional changes**	**Emotional changes**
Confusion and disorientation may mean a person no longer responds to hunger and thirst, so he or she may forget to eat, try to eat non-food items, or not recognise cues for eating, such as a place setting at table, or plate of food **Memory difficulties** interfere with shopping for, preparing and cooking food; keeping to normal mealtime routines; and remembering whether food has been eaten, so that meals may be skipped or eaten more often, and dietary variety diminishes **Concentration difficulties** make it hard to remain focused on tasks connected with shopping, food preparation, cooking, eating and drinking	**Visio-spatial perception changes** interfere with recognising or using cutlery and crockery, and bringing food and drink to the mouth effectively **Sensory perceptions** mean taste can be dulled or changed, interfering with appetite **Oral and dental difficulties** may result in reduced saliva production, problems in chewing to soften food, plus a weakened swallowing reflex, increasing the risk of choking and inhaling food into the lungs, where it can cause pneumonia **Challenging behaviours** caused by damage from dementia to specific areas of the brain can result in hoarding food, sexual disinhibition, restlessness, or anger outbursts at meal times, as well as eating food from others' plates and smearing food **Communication issues** can make it difficult for a person to understand nutritional needs and have preferences understood **Reduced or increased digestive activity** can cause bowel changes, such as constipation or diarrhoea, as well as gastric reflux and indigestion, which make a person less likely to eat **Medication** can cause drowsiness, lack of sensation, taste and other side-effects connected with digestion	**Anxiety** is a common feature of dementia and meal times can increase stress levels, especially if a person feels under pressure to eat, is frightened of choking, or is confused by the surroundings and others' expectations **Agitation** may mean a person cannot sit still and focus on eating, leading to fiddling with the meal setting, getting up and pacing **Depression** commonly accompanies dementia and tends to be under-diagnosed, leading to increasing withdrawal and isolation and reduced appetite **Low motivation** due to depression may lead to inability to manage simple tasks such as providing food and drink for oneself **Paranoia and delusions** can be a feature of dementia and might impact on nutrition if a person believes food is being tampered with or he/she is not worthy to eat it, for example

Case study

Miss Pym worked for the Foreign Office for most of her career and believes the care home where she now lives is a hotel. Most days she tells staff she won't eat lunch because her boss is taking her out for a meal at a local restaurant before an important meeting with foreign government ministers.

1. Which features of dementia are affecting Miss Pym?

2. How would you explain this to a new member of staff?

3. How would you manage this situation?

Your assessment criteria:

DEM 302

1.2 Explain how poor nutrition can contribute to an individual's experience of dementia.

1.3 Outline how other health and emotional conditions may affect the nutritional needs of an individual with dementia.

How does poor nutrition affect people with dementia?

Malnutrition occurs when insufficient foods, or foods with poor nutritional value, are eaten. **Dehydration** is also a common feature of malnutrition, where insufficient fluid is drunk through the day. The key issues caused by poor nutrition are:

• disruption to body systems

• vulnerability to illness and disease.

Disruption to body systems

Food and fluids are essential to the normal functioning of body systems, and a regular intake of a healthy range of food and drinks (see page 189) is necessary to avoid damage and disease. The symptoms of such damage will all be harder for a person with dementia to manage. Dehydration causes symptoms such as a dry mouth, nausea, reduced appetite and **electrolyte imbalance**. This imbalance in turn causes cardiac irregularities and confusion, in addition to the confusion already present from dementia. Without adequate fluid throughout the day, kidney function is reduced, increasing the risk of urinary infections and incontinence. The skin, too, is affected by dehydration. Combined with difficulties managing personal hygiene because of dementia, this can mean that skin becomes sore and could break down.

Vulnerability to illness

A person whose body systems are damaged by malnutrition and dehydration is more vulnerable to infection and less able to fight it. Someone who is ill has a reduced appetite, will be less active, less mobile and has an increased likelihood of further complications. Symptoms of dementia will be magnified and it will be harder to manage the tasks of everyday life. Look at Figure 5.2 opposite, which identifies the negative effects of malnutrition and dehydration.

Key terms

Dehydration: the loss of water and salts essential for normal body function

Electrolyte imbalance: disruption to the levels of essential salts in the body, which impact on body function and can lead to death

Malnutrition: deficiency of nutrients due to inadequate or imbalanced diet, interfering with healthy functioning of the body

Investigate

The Patients Association (www.patients-association.com) produced a leaflet in 2011 entitled 'Malnutrition – how to spot the signs and what to expect from treatment'. Use work, library or internet sources to read through the information and consider how it relates to the individuals you care for.

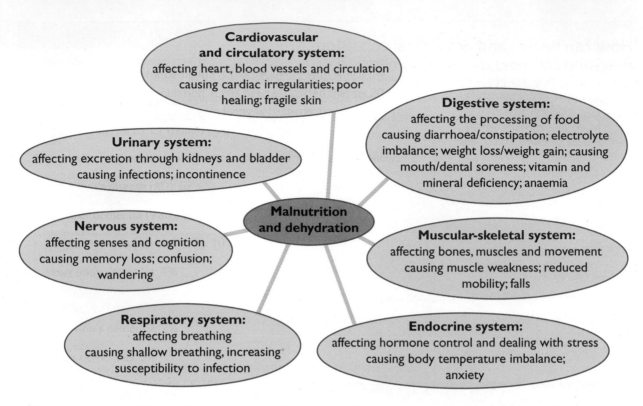

Figure 5.2 Negative effects of malnutrition and dehydration

Case study

Vita has not been eating well since his wife died. He receives a meals service each day, but often forgets to eat his food. Family members notice he has lost weight, and when he falls and breaks his wrist, hospital staff diagnose dehydration as well. Vita finds it hard to cope in the strange surroundings of the ward and calls for his wife constantly.

1. How might a lack of nutrition have increased Vita's vulnerability to falling?

2. How might dementia complicate Vita's health and affect his ability to recover in hospital?

3. If you were caring for Vita, what would you suggest to improve his nutritional status?

? Reflect

The Equality and Human Rights Commission report of November 2011 investigated the home care system in England. It highlighted cases where people unable to feed themselves were given no help and their meals went uneaten. Think about why this might happen in care environments.

Discuss

Share with colleagues what you have noticed about people with dementia who have lost significant weight. Generate some ideas for increasing their calorific intake and improving the nutritional value of meals throughout the day.

How can health and emotional conditions affect nutrition for a person with dementia?

For many older people it is likely that dementia is just one element of a complex health and welfare picture. A common effect of ageing is wear and tear on the body, which can result in increasing illness, disease and disability. Along with physical effects come emotional ones, such as anxiety, frustration, anger, fear about the future and sadness. Think about the impact on nutrition of:

- medical conditions

- health issues

- moods and emotions.

 Key terms

Hyperglycaemia: abnormally high blood sugar

Hypoglycaemia: abnormally low blood sugar

 Reflect

Think about how your different moods affect your appetite and influence what you eat.

 Discuss

Talk with colleagues about individuals you care for who have medical conditions as well as dementia. Consider the ways that the symptoms complicate the person's dementia.

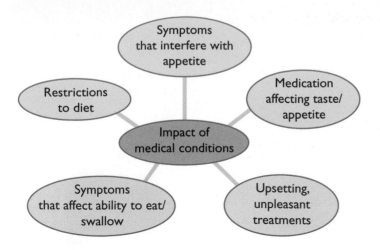

An example of a medical condition affecting nutrition and impacting on dementia is diabetes, where diet must be balanced alongside tablets or insulin injections. People with dementia may forget about dietary restrictions and whether medication has been taken. Symptoms of unstable diabetes, such as hyper- or hypo-glycaemia, may be mistaken for confusion associated with dementia, and go untreated. Consider also the impact of medical conditions such as a stroke, Parkinson's disease and rheumatoid arthritis.

Figure 5.3 The impact of medical conditions on nutrition

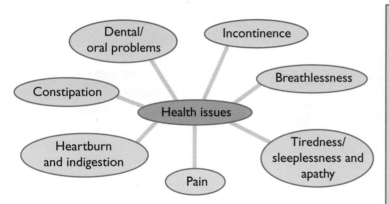

As a person ages, body systems no longer work so efficiently, and the symptoms of this are harder for a person with dementia to recognise, make sense of, communicate and manage. This may have an impact on nutrition. For example, pain may mean a person can't get comfortable to eat, or missing teeth might make it difficult to chew food. Even in hospital or care environments, health issues for people with dementia can go unnoticed.

Figure 5.4 Health issues affecting nutrition

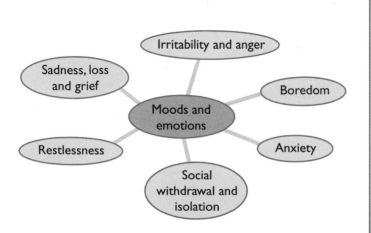

Dementia does not mean people no longer feel emotions, some of which can interfere with wanting to eat and drink. It can be harder for a person with dementia to manage the emotional effects of ageing and know how to seek support. People with insight into their memory loss may avoid friends and family out of embarrassment, and consequent social isolation can reduce dietary intake. A person can become apathetic without stimulus, and is less likely to eat. Anxiety makes it hard for a person to concentrate on food and increases restlessness, which burns more calories, leading to weight loss.

Figure 5.5 Mental health and emotional difficulties affecting nutrition

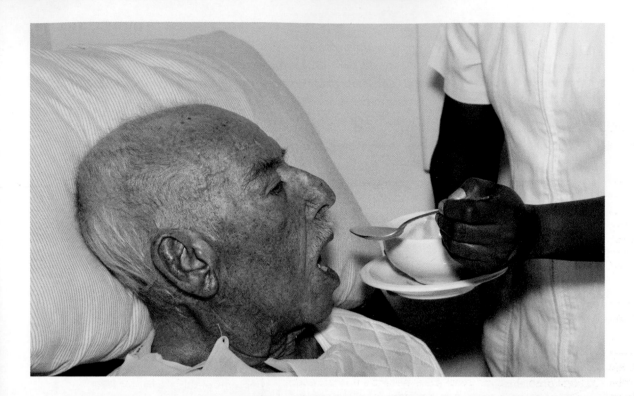

Case study

Sybil has a history of constipation, which is much harder for her to manage now she has dementia and this increases her anxiety. She can never remember if she has passed a motion, so spends a long time straining on the toilet, which has resulted in haemorrhoids (piles). She decides to eat less to reduce the need to go to the toilet, but is becoming more apathetic and less active as a result. Sybil's GP, district nurses and home care team meet to discuss how they can help Sybil.

1. In what ways has dementia impacted on Sybil's ability to manage her constipation?

2. What could be said to Sybil to explain why eating less is not a good solution?

3. Which foods would help Sybil to keep her digestion working well?

 Discuss

Talk together with colleagues about different methods and approaches you use to try to encourage an older person with dementia to eat.

 Investigate

Using library, internet and work sources, find out what you can about dietary fibre, why it is needed and the foods that contain it. You could create a poster of your findings to display at work.

Knowledge Assessment Task

This assessment task covers DEM 302 1.1, 1.2, 1.3.

Dementia impacts on what a person eats and drinks, commonly leading to a poorer nutritional intake. Reduced nutrition has a negative effect on a person's experience of dementia.

To complete this task you need to read each statement in the chart opposite carefully, explain possible reasons for the situation and provide suggestions for managing it.

1. Ellen believes the food in the care home has been tampered with and refuses to eat her meals.

Reason:

Management:

2. Vince finds it harder to concentrate and focus and no longer manages to shop and cook, but his neighbour doesn't mind bringing him small items such as bread and milk, so he mostly eats sandwiches now.

Reason:

Management:

3. Biddy stopped going to the lunch club because she finds it embarrassing when she can't remember people's names, and it doesn't seem worth bothering with a midday meal any more.

Reason:

Management:

4. Derek keeps choking when he's eating, which makes him anxious around meal times.

Reason:

Management:

5. Winston frequently removes his dentures, wraps them in tissues and hides them away, forgetting where he has put them.

Reason:

Management:

Keep the written work that you produce as evidence for your assessment.

> **? Reflect**
>
> *Imagine you lived in a care home. Think about how it would feel to be convinced that someone is against you and might be trying to inflict harm on you in a way that isn't obvious to others. How would this make you feel about eating meals that are cooked by a person you don't know, with foods that you have not shopped for or prepared yourself, in a kitchen you have never seen?*

Why is it important to acknowledge personal and cultural food and drink preferences?

The need to eat and drink is shared by everyone, but the way meals are prepared, the different food types and ways of eating are influenced by a person's background and likes and dislikes. Personal and cultural preferences take on greater significance for a person with dementia, because they help to trigger memories and provide a familiar structure and routine. This gives each person a sense of unique individuality. Factors to consider are set out in the table below.

Figure 5.6 Cultural and personal food and drink preferences

Term	Preference	Example
Ethnicity	Foods usual to a country/region; food prepared and eaten according to custom	Agnes is Scottish and has had porridge with salt and no sugar or milk for breakfast since she was a child
Religion	Prohibited foods; specific preparation of foods; particular food for religious occasions	A Kosher diet is given to Ben, who is Jewish: meat is prepared according to custom and certain foods are included or excluded
Beliefs	Vegetarian, vegan	Marnie is given rissoles made with lentils as a vegetarian alternative to meat
Culture/background	Social and family routines; celebration meals (these link to the power of reminiscence to whet appetites)	Because Rick's family used to eat tea in front of the television on Sundays, the care home arrange for his wife to continue this practice and he always eats really well
Individual taste	Likes and dislikes	Fish was never a favourite of Pete's, even though he was a fisherman for 30 years

The importance of meeting dietary preferences

The main reason for finding out about food preferences is that people are more likely to eat and drink well if they are enjoying their meal, but there are additional benefits as well. These are set out in the diagram opposite (figure 5.7).

Your assessment criteria:

DEM 302

1.4 Explain the importance of recognising and meeting an individual's personal and cultural preferences for food and drink.

Key terms

Culture: beliefs and ways of behaving that are characteristic of a particular social, ethnic, or age group

Institutionalisation: the process of conforming to the routines and usual behaviours expected within an institution and suppressing individuality

Discuss

Talk with colleagues about routines to do with meal times that take place where you work. Discuss whether these have the potential to ignore the personal preferences of individuals.

Figure 5.7 Reasons for meeting dietary preferences

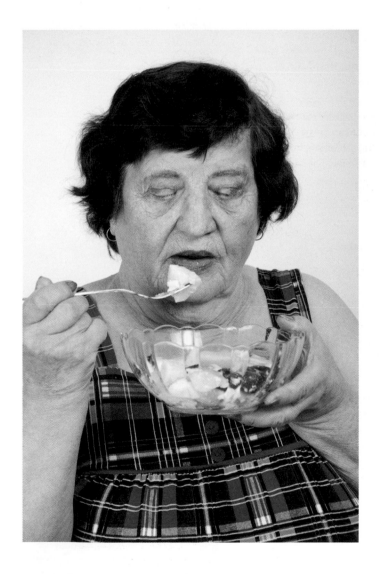

Investigate

Using internet and library sources, find out about traditions related to food from different countries. Consider such matters as communal eating with fingers out of a shared bowl; use of chopsticks; rituals related to religious festivals.

Reflect

Think about traditions and rituals associated with food that took place when you were a child.

Finding out about the preferences of a person with dementia

A person with dementia may have difficulty identifying preferences and communicating these verbally. It is important for care workers to encourage a person with dementia to express his or her wishes and notice the meals that appear to be enjoyed. Speak also with family about their relative's likes and dislikes, recording the information for all staff members including the person doing the cooking. Be specific. For example, if a person likes fish, find out which meals containing fish are preferred. Also, check whether individuals want to try something new, because tastes can change and sometimes the dulling of taste and smell associated with dementia can mean a person needs more strongly flavoured, highly seasoned food.

Case study

Bettina is from Portugal, and as her dementia progresses she stops speaking English and reverts to Portuguese. All day she paces the corridors of the care home, where staff constantly try to persuade her to sit down. She doesn't usually settle, even to eat or drink, until late evening, long after the last meal has been served. The manager is concerned because at the monthly weight check Bettina has lost 2 kg.

1. How can staff reflect something of Bettina's cultural background in the care they offer around food and meal times?

2. How might staff increase Bettina's nutritional intake?

3. What observations should staff be making to monitor the situation?

Why is it important to provide nutritional variety?

Most people prefer to eat a varied diet, but variety is also necessary to provide a range of nutritional elements that are contained in different food types and required for healthy functioning. Consider:

- balanced menu choice

- stimulating appetite

- food combinations for optimum nutrition

- food fortification and supplements.

Your assessment criteria:

DEM 302

1.5 Explain why it is important to include a variety of food and drink in the diet of an individual with dementia.

Investigate

Using library, Internet and work sources, find out more about vitamins, such as vitamins A, B12, C and D, and how these contribute to the functioning of the body. Find out which foods contain these vitamins and make a table to illustrate your findings.

Providing a balanced menu

People need a balance of different nutrients in their diet. The range of these is illustrated in the diagram below (figure 5.8). If you help a person with dementia to shop and cook, you need to balance nutritional advice about what to buy alongside food preferences. For example, a person may not like (or be unable to chew) vegetables or fruit, which would reduce the intake of vitamins, minerals and fibre. But the person may be happy to eat these puréed to form soup or pulped in a smoothie.

In care environments, spend time helping a person select items from the menu, bearing in mind that something chosen in advance may not be remembered when the meal arrives. It may help to write choices on a calendar, or use pictures of meals as a memory and communication aid.

? Reflect

Think about foods that might be good to tempt a person's appetite after they have been unwell or when they're feeling upset.

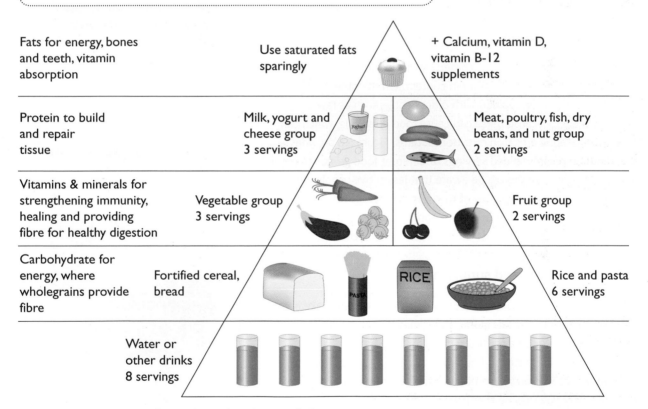

Fats for energy, bones and teeth, vitamin absorption — Use saturated fats sparingly — + Calcium, vitamin D, vitamin B-12 supplements

Protein to build and repair tissue — Milk, yogurt and cheese group 3 servings — Meat, poultry, fish, dry beans, and nut group 2 servings

Vitamins & minerals for strengthening immunity, healing and providing fibre for healthy digestion — Vegetable group 3 servings — Fruit group 2 servings

Carbohydrate for energy, where wholegrains provide fibre — Fortified cereal, bread — RICE — Rice and pasta 6 servings

Water or other drinks 8 servings

Figure 5.8 How to provide nutritional variety each day.
Remember that some foods contain combined nutritional value,
such as cheese, which is fat and protein

💬 Discuss

Talk together with colleagues about designing menu plans that include balanced and nutritious meals suitable for an older person with dementia.

Stimulating appetite

If a meal is enjoyable it is more likely to be eaten. Stimulating the senses increases appetite, so consider delicious aromas, interesting textures, the sizzle of something frying and the sight of steam wafting from saucepans, all of which increase anticipation. Helping a person pour a drink from a jug involves touch and the sound of liquid pouring or ice cubes chinking, which can stimulate a person to drink. Flavouring water with cordial makes it more palatable for some. It may be appropriate to offer an alcoholic drink such as a Sherry before meals, but check whether this is desired and compatible with medication. Using a toaster is a simple way in which people can benefit from seeing and smelling food in preparation. Brief and gentle exercise before meal times also increases appetite and makes a person feel ready to eat.

Optimising nutrition

The benefits of nutrition are increased by making sure food is not overcooked, which destroys vitamin content. On the other hand some foods should be avoided with older people, such as raw or underdone eggs, because these can cause food poisoning, which can have a devastating effect on nutritional status. Figure 5.8 provides guidelines on recommended servings of different food groups to provide optimum nutrition, although be aware that less active people need less carbohydrate. Eight glasses of fluid per day (unless restricted due to another medical condition, such as congestive heart failure) are recommended, but can include drinks other than water.

Food fortification and supplements

Sometimes it is not possible for a person with dementia to take in adequate nutrition in meals alone, and it may be necessary to use supplementary feeding to fortify the diet. Supplements come in different forms, illustrated in figure 5.9 opposite. These should only be used after consultation with a doctor or dietician/nutritionist. Be aware that as a carer you may be the first person to recognise that a person is not eating or drinking well, and it is your responsibility to bring it to the attention of your manager, who can refer the person to a specialist practitioner (see page 196).

Key term

Supplementary feeding: programme in which food is provided to individuals specifically to prevent or treat malnutrition

Investigate

Using library, internet and work sources, find out more about vitamins, such as vitamins A, B12, C and D, and how these contribute to the functioning of the body. Find out which foods contain these vitamins and make a table to illustrate your findings.

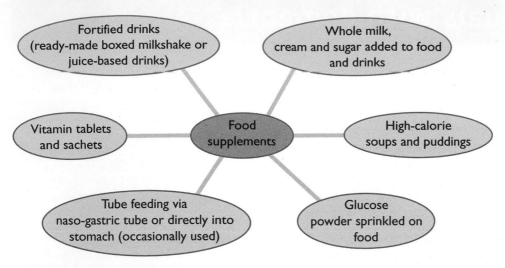

Figure 5.9 Methods of fortifying diet

Knowledge Assessment Task

This assessment task covers DEM 302 1.4, 1.5.

Meals provided for older people with dementia need to reflect a person's cultural and personal preferences while also providing a varied and nutritionally balanced diet. Design a whole day's menu including drinks and breakfast, lunch, dinner, morning and afternoon snack for the following individuals, explaining your choices.

1. *Bert has traditional tastes, enjoying old-fashioned food from his childhood. He is the son of a dairy farmer and says his mother cooked plain food and made lovely pastry and cakes. Luckily Bert is not overweight, and as he walks a lot he has a hearty appetite.*

2. *Mrs Patel has been off her food since she had flu. She has lost weight and will only tolerate small amounts of food through the day, sometimes wanting only a drink or snack rather than a full meal. Her family say she prefers eating traditional meals from southern India and does not really like Western food.*

3. *Lexi is always ready for her breakfast and eats well at this time of day, but staff at the care home find it hard to persuade her to sit and eat for other meals, and often leave finger food for her to take as she passes.*

Keep the written work that you produce as evidence for your assessment.

 Investigate

Using internet, local community and work sources, find out about the provision of meal services at home in your area and the ways they ensure nutritional value, balance and variety.

? Reflect

Think about going out to restaurants and favourite dishes you enjoy. Identify the elements of the food and service that add to your enjoyment. Consider whether you could incorporate some of these touches where you work.

 Discuss

Talk with colleagues about the menu choice provided to the individuals you care for. Consider the nutritional variety and balance, and suggest ways to enhance this.

In what ways can meal times create barriers to healthy eating?

Meal times can be a barrier preventing a person with dementia from eating a healthy diet, whether at home or in a communal environment. Look at the table (figure 5.10) below, which highlights how this can happen.

Figure 5.10 Negative aspects of communal versus individual meal times

Communal meal times	Individual meal times
Can be noisy and distracting if a person with dementia is easily over-stimulated and unable to concentrate on eating a meal with others	People with dementia can become isolated and may not bother to shop, cook or eat regularly; appetite may decrease; there may be a lack of nutritional variety; poor food hygiene may lead to food poisoning
It can be stressful for a person with dementia to meet the social expectations of others, such as acceptable manners and following conversations	Lone individuals with dementia cannot observe and follow the example of others eating around the table
The rigidity of a meal eaten together at a specific time does not allow for a person with dementia to eat when they please or when they feel hungry	There are no prompts such as a dining table laid ready for a meal with place settings, flowers or other decorations, especially when celebrating events such as birthdays
It can be embarrassing for a person who needs aids to eat food and who may drop food or dribble	There is no stimulus to appetite such as seeing meals set down on the table and witnessing others enjoying their food
Some people with dementia need to 'graze' – that is, eat small amounts of food while moving around, or getting up and down during a meal	Without prompts, meals provided by a meal delivery service may be forgotten or unfinished

Your assessment criteria:

DEM 302

2.1 Describe how mealtime cultures and environments can be a barrier to meeting the nutritional needs of an individual with dementia.

2.2 Describe how mealtime environments and food presentation can be designed to help an individual to eat and drink.

 Investigate

Ask your manager if you can experiment with playing different types of music during meal times to see whether certain music, or radio stations, or no music, encourages eating.

Case study

Bridie was a sociable person before her stroke, which resulted in vascular dementia. She is embarrassed by the need to feed herself with a spoon and that she drops food. She also dribbles and has a weakened swallowing reflex. Although Bridie asks to have her meals in her room, staff prefer her to eat at a communal dining table where they can help her quickly if she chokes.

1. What would you do to reconcile the conflicting wishes of staff and resident in this situation?

2. What are your reasons for these decisions?

3. How would you arrange the dining environment to meet Bridie's needs more effectively?

? Reflect

Think about different environments where you enjoy eating meals, perhaps outdoor picnics or breakfast in bed, and consider whether these ideas might work for those you care for.

💬 Discuss

Talk with colleagues about the various aids you use when helping people with dementia to eat, and share what you have found most useful for particular individuals and circumstances.

How can the environment and food presentation encourage eating and drinking?

There are positive steps you can take to improve the intake of food and drink for individuals with dementia. Consider:

- conducive mealtime environments

- food presentation.

Conducive mealtime environments

The surroundings for eating can be as important as the food that is provided. Be flexible in your thinking, and remember that individuals with dementia may wish to eat some meals at the dining table and others in bed, or from a tray on their lap. Some may eat standing up, or while moving. Also be flexible with timings, because set meal times may no longer have meaning for people with dementia, who might wish to eat when they feel like it or when they are hungry.

Be sensitive when you are seating groups of people together. Allow for choice of company to be expressed and make sure individuals and their specific needs are compatible with each other. For example, don't sit two restless people together or they will be easily distracted. It can help to have staff members eating a meal alongside individuals with dementia, their example providing prompts about using cutlery and drinking and eating well. People will eat more successfully if they feel relaxed and stress free.

Think about the physical surroundings in a dining area. Make sure it is warm and light. Provide information, such as signs that state it is a dining area, perhaps with a clock-face to show the time of the next meal. A menu (preferably illustrated) provides a prompt and helps to prepare a person for eating a meal. Items related to eating also nudge the memory, such as crockery displayed on a dresser, tablecloths and napkins. Show thoughtfulness by displaying flowers or candles, out of reach of those who may harm themselves. Look at figure 5.11 to remind yourself of each factor to consider.

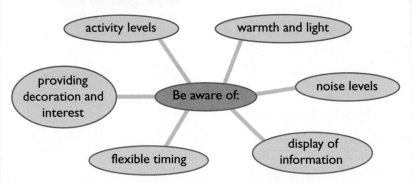

Figure 5.11 Creating conducive mealtime environments

Range of food presentations

The way that food is presented impacts on eating, and an attractive-looking plate can stimulate appetite. A huge portion of food can be off-putting, whereas a smaller portion, presented carefully, looks appetising. A garnish of salad, fruit or herbs is an attractive finish that shows attention to detail. As well as presenting a meal attractively, always provide appropriate sauces and seasoning.

According to the needs of a person with dementia, some meals need to be presented differently to enable an individual to eat safely. Look at the diagram (figure 5.12 opposite).

- A soft diet shouldn't require chewing, and includes foods that can be eaten with a fork or spoon alone, such as mashed potatoes.

- Puréed food is required by someone with a weak swallowing reflex. Always liquidise different food types separately to preserve their original colour, making sure you let the person know what the meal consists of, because this may not be obvious.

- The consistency of drinks and some foods, such as soup and puddings, may need to be thickened to provide bulk for someone who is likely to choke.

- Chopping food may help a person with dementia to eat independently, but do this in the kitchen to avoid embarrassment.

- Finger foods such as sandwiches and bite-size items can be eaten without cutlery. This is an advantage for people whose cognitive and functional skills are affected, but who wish to eat independently without drawing attention to their difficulty.

Discuss

Talk together with colleagues about ways to ensure that a person with dementia who is restless can still manage to eat enough calories to prevent weight loss.

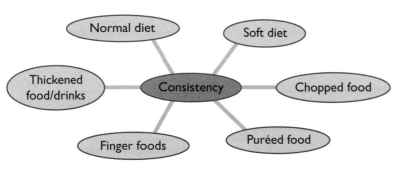

Figure 5.12 Food and drink consistencies

Case study

The manager of The Pines care home wants to create a reminiscence dining area. The average age of the residents means they mostly grew up and had their families in the 1940s and 1950s.

1. What do you think might be the reasons for the manager's decision?

2. What sort of items do you think might fit in a 1940s and 1950s reminiscence dining room?

3. What ideas about dining room design do you have to encourage people with dementia to eat?

 Investigate

Using library and internet sources, gather together information about indoor and outdoor plants that can be grown in pots and bear fruit that can be eaten, such as tomatoes, cress and lettuces. These types of plants can be tended and eaten by residents in a care home or at a day centre.

How do you support the needs and abilities of individuals when they eat and drink?

It is important to organise meal times in ways that meet the specific needs and support the abilities of each individual you provide care for. Think particularly about:

• meal planning

• addressing needs and supporting abilities.

Meal planning

A regular timetable of meals, snacks and drinks will not necessarily suit each person with dementia, and it is important to tailor occasions for eating and drinking to the individual, rather than making them fit into a programme that suits you.

This flexible approach means you need to be sensitive to the best times, ways and environments to offer food and drink. Look at the diagram below (figure 5.14), which sets out the questions you need to be asking about each person for whom you provide care.

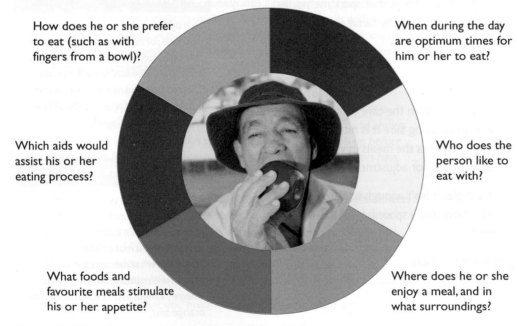

How does he or she prefer to eat (such as with fingers from a bowl)?

When during the day are optimum times for him or her to eat?

Which aids would assist his or her eating process?

Who does the person like to eat with?

What foods and favourite meals stimulate his or her appetite?

Where does he or she enjoy a meal, and in what surroundings?

Figure 5.14 Person-centred approach to meal planning

Case study

Frankie Ford worked in a fairground from the age of 14 until his twenties. The care workers discover this when someone mentions candy floss over the lunch table.

Frankie, who doesn't often say much, suddenly shouts out 'candy floss, toffee apples, fish 'n' chips and vinegar, whelks in a jar – that tickles my fancy!', and roars with laughter.

1. How can care workers use this information from Frankie's past?

2. How would you make sure this information was passed on?

3. How would you respond to a person who judges these foods to be 'nutritionally bad'?

Investigate

Find out whether there is a nutrition and nutritional screening policy where you work. If there is, read it and make sure you understand it. If there isn't, ask your manager about this.

Addressing needs and supporting abilities

It is just as important to recognise a person's abilities as it is to identify disabilities, so that you can build on strengths and help a person to remain independent for as long as possible. Look at the guidelines for addressing needs and supporting abilities in figure 5.15 below.

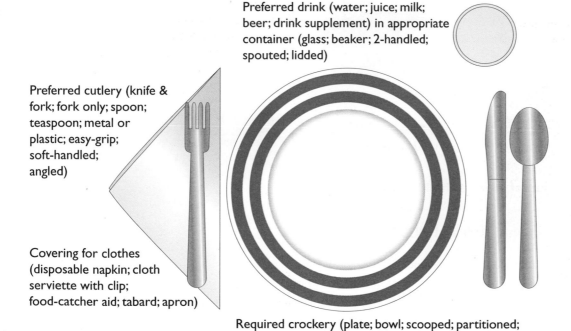

Preferred drink (water; juice; milk; beer; drink supplement) in appropriate container (glass; beaker; 2-handled; spouted; lidded)

Preferred cutlery (knife & fork; fork only; spoon; teaspoon; metal or plastic; easy-grip; soft-handled; angled)

Covering for clothes (disposable napkin; cloth serviette with clip; food-catcher aid; tabard; apron)

Required crockery (plate; bowl; scooped; partitioned; high-sided; coloured border) on mat (ordinary or non-slip) with necessary aids (plate guard; heat-proof plate)

Figure 5.15 Guidelines for addressing needs and supporting abilities

How can you identify the positive effect of a person-centred approach on nutrition?

It is important to assess the impact of the care you give, to check it is meeting the needs and improving the wellbeing of each individual. To establish whether a person-centred approach is having a positive effect on nutrition you should consider:

- indicators of wellbeing

- weight measurements, BMI and MUST.

Indicators of wellbeing

It is important to observe, record and track a range of indicators for healthy nutrition. There is a danger too many charts can shift your attention from the person to the process of form-filling, so use the information you record to guide the care you give.

Your assessment criteria:

DEM 302

3.4 Demonstrate how a person-centred approach to meeting nutritional requirements has improved the wellbeing of an individual with dementia.

Discuss

Discuss how to design a survey for service users and their family members to find out their opinions on menus, mealtime environments and practice.

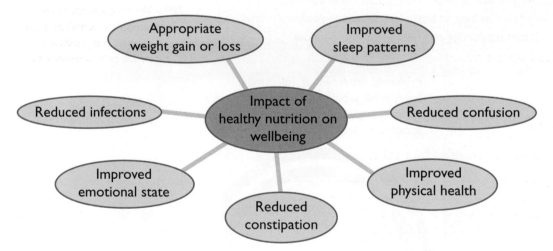

Figure 5.16 Indicators of improved health and wellbeing

Weight measurements, BMI and MUST

Weighing a person is a straightforward method of checking whether weight is stable. Doing this regularly allows comparisons to be made over time. The Body Mass Index (BMI) system looks at height and weight measurements together, compared across populations, and provides a scale indicating if a person is underweight (BMI under 18.5) or overweight (BMI over 30).

It may not be possible to weigh individuals in their own home, and some are unable to stand and balance sufficiently to use scales. In these cases you can use circumference measurements around the upper arm. This process is explained within a tool referred to as MUST, the Malnutrition Universal Screening Tool system. Information about this commonly used assessment tool will probably be available where you work, or can be accessed from the internet.

Investigate

Using work or internet sources, find out as much as you can about the MUST screening tool. Try it out on yourself to practise how to carry out the calculations accurately.

Case study

During a recent inspection of Balinrees care home, concern was expressed about the physical wellbeing of three residents who had each lost a significant amount of weight since admission. In response, the manager points out that measurements of weight were taken each month, the completed records proving there was no negligence.

1. In what ways do you think there might have been negligence?

2. Who would you inform if a person's weight measurements were changing?

3. What actions can be taken to stop unwanted weight loss, and how would you monitor progress?

Reflect

How do you usually assess your own nutritional health? Think about the fit of your clothes; the appearance of skin, hair and nails; your energy levels; the way you feel about food and eating.

Discuss

Talk with colleagues about the different kinds of records that help you to keep track of a person's nutritional health and wellbeing.

Practical Assessment Task

This assessment task covers DEM 302 3.1, 3.4.

To be an effective care worker you must find out about each person as a unique individual and apply the information to provide a diet that suits preferences, meets nutritional requirements and improves wellbeing. To carry out this task you need to do the following.

1. *Select a person you work with who has dementia.*

2. *Create, or build on, a life story to highlight those elements that relate to dietary needs and preferences.*

3. *Write a care plan or draw a diagram that shows how you apply this information in practice to provide a diet that meets the nutritional requirements and personal preferences of the individual.*

4. *With reference to figure 5.16 opposite, provide evidence to show that wellbeing is improved by your interventions.*

Your evidence for this task must be based on your practice in a real work environment and must be presented in a format acceptable to your assessor.

Practical Assessment Task

This assessment task covers DEM 302 3.2, 3.3.

The mealtime environment and support for the abilities of each individual to eat and drink are as important as providing a healthy diet. Using the same person as for the previous task and with reference to figure 5.15 on page 201, carry out the following task.

1. *Draw your own meal setting plan to show how you intend to:*
   * *manage meal-, snack- and drink-time environments during a day for this person*
   * *support the person's eating and drinking abilities.*

2. *Identify the person's strengths and how you will build on these.*

3. *Identify aids and interventions required.*

Your evidence for this task must be based on your practice in a real work environment and must be presented in a format acceptable to your assessor.

Assessment checklist

The assessment of this unit is partly knowledge-based (assessing things you need to know about) and partly competence-based (assessing things you need to do in the real work environment). To complete this unit successfully, you will need to produce evidence of both your knowledge and your competence.

The knowledge-based assessment criteria for DEM 302 are listed in the 'What you need to know' table below. The practical or competence-based criteria for DEM 302 are listed in the 'What you need to do' table below. Your tutor or assessor will help you to prepare for your assessment, and the tasks suggested in the chapter will help you to create the evidence you need.

Assessment criteria	What you need to know	Assessment task
DEM 302		
1.1	Describe how cognitive, functional and emotional changes associated with dementia can affect eating, drinking and nutrition	Page 184
1.2	Explain how poor nutrition can contribute to an individual's experience of dementia	Page 184
1.3	Outline how other health and emotional conditions may affect the nutritional needs of an individual with dementia	Page 184
1.4	Explain the importance of recognising and meeting an individual's personal and cultural preferences for food and drink	Page 191
1.5	Explain why it is important to include a variety of food and drink in the diet of an individual with dementia	Page 191
2.1	Describe how mealtime cultures and environments can be a barrier to meeting the nutritional needs of an individual with dementia	Page 198
2.2	Describe how mealtime environments and food presentation can be designed to help an individual to eat and drink	Page 198
2.3	Describe how a person-centred approach can support an individual, with dementia at different levels of ability, to eat and drink	Page 198

Assessment criteria	What you need to do	Assessment task
3.1	Demonstrate how the knowledge of life history of an individual with dementia has been used to provide a diet that meets his/her preferences	Page 203
3.2	Demonstrate how meal times for an individual with dementia are planned to support his/her ability to eat and drink	Page 204
3.3	Demonstrate how the specific eating and drinking abilities and needs of an individual with dementia have been addressed	Page 204
3.4	Demonstrate how a person-centred approach to meeting nutritional requirements has improved the wellbeing of an individual with dementia	Page 203

Services and organisations

The organisations listed below provide information, guidance and a range of care and support services that address the needs of individuals with dementia as well as the people who provide care and support for them. (All information correct at time of going to press.)

Organisation	Website	Description
Alzheimer's Association	www.alz.org/AboutAD/Stages.asp	The leading USA-based voluntary organisation for information on Alzheimer's care
Alzheimer's Disease International	www.alz.co.uk/carers/yourself.html	An umbrella organisation representing Alzheimer's organisations around the world. It seeks to raise awareness of Alzheimer's and other causes of dementia
Alzheimer's Research UK	www.alzheimers-research.org.uk	The leading UK charity of research into the cure, prevention and treatment of Alzheimer's and other forms of dementia
Alzheimer Scotland	www.alzscot.org/	The leading voluntary organisation in Scotland that supports and works on behalf of people with dementia, their carers and families
Alzheimer Scotland: Dementia Rights	www.dementiarights.org	Alzheimer Scotland's campaign for the rights of people with dementia and their carers. The site includes lots of useful information about equality, rights and discrimination that applies to the UK as well as Scotland
Alzheimer's Society	www.alzheimers.org.uk/site/index.php	A leading UK research and care charity for people with dementia, their families and carers
AT Dementia	www.atdementia.org.uk	Information on assistive technology for people with dementia
Bradford Dementia Group	www.brad.ac.uk/acad/health/dementia	Information about research, education and training that aims to improve quality of life and care for people with dementia and their families
Dementia Advocacy Support Network (DASN) International	www.dasninternational.org	A global support network that promotes respect, dignity and support for people with dementia

Organisation	Website	Description
Dementia Awareness	www.dementiaawareness.co.uk	A group that campaigns to raise awareness of dementia. The site provides useful information and valuable insights into the experiences of individuals with dementia and their carers
Dementia Cafe	www.dementiacentre.com	An online space for people with dementia, their families and carers as well as professionals. The site allows you to give and receive information and support about dementia-related issues
Dementia UK	www.dementiauk.com	This website promotes and seeks to develop the work of Admiral Nurses in the UK. These are specialist nurses who focus on meeting the needs of the carers and families of individuals with dementia
Mental Health Foundation	www.mentalhealth.org.uk/information/mental-health-a-z/dementia/	This site provides information and resources about dementia and care-related issues
National Institute of Clinical Excellence (NICE)	www.nice.org.uk	This organisation provides information about standards and best practice in dementia care. To find out more, type 'Dementia' into the website's search feature
NHS Choices	www.nhs.uk	Information and links to other sites on a wide range of health and care issues that are relevant to people with dementia and their families
Royal College of Nursing	www.rcn.org.uk	This organisation represents nurses and nursing and provides a range of information and publications on or relevant to dementia care issues
Social Care Institute for Excellence (SCIE)	www.scie.org.uk/publications/dementia	An independent charity that works with a range of vulnerable individuals, carers and service providers to raise awareness of social care issues. SCIE campaign on dementia care issues and produce a range of useful publications
Talking Point	http://forum.alzheimers.org.uk/forum.php	The Alzheimer's Society online forum for individuals with dementia, their carers and family members

Further reading

Further reading on a wide variety of issues covered in this handbook can be found in the publications listed below.

Adams T. and Clarke C. L. (Eds) *Dementia Care: Developing Partnerships in Practice*. Bailliere Tindall 1999

Bartle, C. *Knowledge Set for Dementia*. Heinemann 2007

Bayley, J. *Iris: A Memoir of Iris Murdoch*. Abacus 1999

Bhugra, D. and Bahl, V. *Ethnicity: An Agenda for Mental Health*. Gaskell 1999

Bryden, C. *Dancing with Dementia*. Jessica Kingsley 2005

Davis, R. *My Journey into Alzheimer's Disease*. Tyndale House 1989

Downs, M. *Excellence in Dementia Care*. Open University Press 2008

Feil, N. *The Validation Breakthrough*. Barnes and Noble 2002

Friel-McGowin, D. *Living in the Labyrinth: A Personal Journey Through the Maze of Alzheimer's Disease*. Delacorte Press 1993

Goldsmith, M. *Hearing the Voice of People with Dementia: Opportunities and Obstacles*. Jessica Kingsley 1996

Kerr, D. *Understanding Learning Disabilities and Dementia – Developing Effective Interventions*. Jessica Kingsley 2005

Killick, J. and Allan, K. *Communication and the Care of Older People with Dementia*. Open University Press 2002

Kitwood, T. *Dementia Reconsidered*. Open University Press 1997

Morris, G. and Morris, J. *The Dementia Care Workbook*. Open University Press/McGraw Hill 2010

Pritchard, J. *Good Practice in the Law and Safeguarding Adults – Criminal Justice and Adult Protection*. Jessica Kingsley 2008

Schweitzer, P. and Bruce, E. *Remembering Yesterday, Caring Today – Reminiscence in Dementia Care: A Guide to Good Practice*. Jessica Kingsley 2008

Social Care Institute for Excellence, *Assessing the Mental Health Needs of Older People*. www.scie.org.uk/publications 2006

Sutcliffe, D. *Introducing Dementia – The Essential Facts and Issues of Care*. Age Concern England 2001

Index

abilities 98, 122, 200–1

abuse 30–1, 41, 168

active listening 40, 68, 69, 96, 99

activities 9, 36, 43, 103, 115, 120, 126

adaptations 107, 118, 119

administration of medication 141, 145, 149–52, 154

Admiral nurses 27, 28, 47

adverse reactions to medication 137, 142–3, 145, 158, 159, 168, 171

    see also side effects

advocacy 60, 168

advocates 18–19, 27, 36, 43, 47–8, 124

age 92–3

age-related memory impairment 12, 14–15

aggression 19, 26, 28, 58, 89, 100

    minimising 41, 97

agnosia 54

agreed ways of working 108, 113

    medication 139, 138, 153, 155, 161, 166, 171

aids

    to communication 71

    to eating and drinking 196, 197, 198, 201

    see also adaptations

alertness 21, 36

Alzheimer's disease 20, 25, 26, 28

ampoules 151

anger 57, 90, 179, 182, 183

anti-depressants 142, 143

anti-psychotic medication 141, 142, 143–4

anxiety 72, 179, 181, 182, 183

apathy 12, 142, 143, 183, 184

aphasia 54

appetite, stimulating 189–90, 192

aromas (food) 190, 199

artefacts 62, 116

as required (PRN) medication 141, 162–3

assessment checklists 50–1, 78–9, 128–31, 173–5, 205

assessment of needs 18, 49

assistive technologies 42, 118, 119, 121

    see also adaptations; aids

assumptions about dementia 88–9, 91

attitudes

    to dementia 30–1, 88–91

    enabling 122

audiologists 75

autonomy 156, 158, 159

balanced menu 188–9

behaviour of others 30–1

behavioural changes 8, 11, 22, 26

behavioural triggers 74

beliefs 86, 116, 120, 186

beneficence 158, 159

biographies see life stories

biomedical model of dementia 16–17, 88, 89

BME (black and minority ethnic) communities 25, 94

BMI (Body Mass Index) 202–3

BNF (British National Formulary) 144, 165, 169

body language 65, 66, 67–8, 71

    see also non-verbal communication

Body Mass Index (BMI) 202–3

brain, dementia and 10–11, 16, 20–1, 22

British National Formulary (BNF) 144, 165, 169

capacity, mental 18–19, 47–8, 106, 107, 110, 139

care

    involving individuals in 37–9, 42–3

    organisation of 89, 164–5

    in the past 88–9

    positive attitudes to 90–1

care homes 30, 101, 114–15, 116, 118

    see also residential care settings

care plans 73

carers 44–5, 85, 88, 99, 158, 159

    common anxieties 123

    involvement of 44, 101, 124–5

    legal rights 124

    needs of 48–9, 108

    and restriction of independence 125

    support for 44, 49, 108, 123, 124, 125–7

    see also families; partners

caring relationship 44–5

causes of dementia 20–3

cerebro-vascular accidents see strokes

choices 32, 36, 104–5, 106–11, 121, 126, 193

    food and drink 187

    restriction of 125

    see also preferences

choking 18, 179, 189, 192, 195, 196, 198

cognitive enhancement 141, 142, 143

cognitive function, person centred care and 98

cognitive impairment 11, 12, 13, 88, 97, 141

    and nutrition 178, 179, 197

comfort 72, 75

communication 9, 31, 103, 110

    factors influencing 54–8

    with learning disabled people 96

    methods 40–1

    non-verbal see non-verbal communication

    person-centred 59–64

    problems 12, 22, 72, 179

    style 40–1, 61, 65, 66

    supporting 71–6

    techniques 40–1, 61, 65, 68–9

    verbal 55–6, 65, 96, 110, 120

    see also language

communication boards 68, 69

communication passports 72, 73–4

community care support 18

community psychiatric nurses (CPNs) 27, 28, 72

concentration 8, 12, 22, 55, 179

confidentiality 44, 45, 73, 108

    medication 153, 156, 158, 159

confusion 8, 12, 13, 21, 22, 88, 180, 183

    delirium 13

    nutrition and 179, 180, 181, 202

    reducing 120, 121, 202

congruence 32, 33

consent to medication 146, 154, 156, 158, 159, 160

constipation 179, 181, 183, 184, 202

nausea 57
needles 151–2, 159
needs 18, 32, 33–4, 35–6, 89, 98–101, 116
  of carers 48–9, 108
  daily living 100
  eating and drinking 200–1
  nutritional 178–91
  personal care 94, 100, 112, 121
needs assessment 18, 49
  of carers 49, 108
neglect 30–1, 168
  self-neglect 18
neuroleptics 142
neuroprotection 141, 142
No Secrets, Adult Protection 108
non-verbal communication 54, 66, 71, 89, 96, 97, 99, 110, 120
  emphasising 65, 67–8
  recognising 40–1, 72, 105
  sign language 65, 69, 73
nurses 72
nutrition
  balanced menu 188–91
  effects of dementia on 178–85
  emotions and 178, 179, 182, 183, 202
  food and drink preferences 38, 99, 186–8, 199
  health conditions and 182–5
  indicators 202–3
  mealtime environments 192–8
  and medication 179, 182, 190
  supporting good nutrition 199–204
  see also diet; dietary supplements; food
nutritional status 178
nutritional variety 188–91, 192
observation 57–8, 99
occupational therapists 27, 72, 119, 196
oral difficulties 179, 181, 183, 196
organisation of care 89, 164–5
other professionals 46–9, 101
others, behaviour of 30–1
'over the counter' remedies 146–8
pain 18, 57, 72, 162, 183
pain relief 137, 141, 162–3
paranoia 56, 57, 178, 179
parenteral medication 151
Parkinson's disease 25, 57, 183

partners 43, 98, 124, 125, 126, 127
  and confidentiality 45, 73
  and life stories 37, 99, 116
  see also carers; families
patience 60
patient information leaflets 154
person centred approach 30, 31, 32–9, 88, 89, 90–1, 98, 126
  to communication 59–64
  dementia as a disability model 18
  to eating and drinking 196–8
  and inclusion 102–5
  for learning disabled people 96
  to medication 161
  to nutrition 202–3
  role of carers 44–5, 44–6
  safeguarding individuals 106
personal care 38, 94, 121–2, 125
  needs and preferences 94, 100, 112, 121
  privacy 104, 112–14, 121
personal comfort 75
personal environment 114–15, 116
personal hygiene 20, 23, 38, 104, 121, 180
personal information 37–9, 75
personal protective equipment 121
personal space 114–15
personality 39, 57, 61, 62
  changes 8, 88, 89
personhood 36
pharmacy medicines 137
photographs 31, 38, 41, 62, 66, 116
physical environment 57, 58, 118–20
physical exercise 120
physical health 57–8, 202
physiotherapists 73, 196
Pick's disease 20, 22
pictures 31, 38, 62, 66, 114, 116, 119
  of food and meals 189, 199
plants 195
POMs (prescription only medicines) 137, 140
positive attitudes to dementia care 90–1
positive reinforcement 120, 122
postural hypotension 143
potential 34
  supporting individuals to achieve 118–22
practitioners 71–3, 101, 107

behaviour of 30–1
  and medication 145–6, 169
  and nutrition 196
  role of others 46–9
preferences 32, 74, 98–101
  food and drink 38, 99, 186–8, 199
  personal care 94, 100, 112, 121
prescription administration charts 152
prescription only medicines (POMs) 137, 140
prevalence rates 9, 24, 25
privacy 31, 36, 104, 115, 156, 160
  personal care 112–14, 121
PRN (pro re nata) medication 141, 162–3
problem-solving skills 21
professionals 71–3, 101, 107
  and medication 145–6, 169
  and nutrition 196
  role of 46–9
prognosis 123
psychiatrists 27
psychologists 27
quality of life 27, 28, 96, 119, 143
rapport 59
reality orientation 66, 69
recall problems 26
receiving supplies of medication 153
recognition 9, 10, 14, 30
records, of nutritional health 203
records of administration (medication) 171
referring to others 48–9
relatives see families
religious beliefs 94
  and food and drink 94, 99, 186
  and personal care 94, 121
reminiscence therapy 38–9
reminiscences 38–9, 62, 66, 69, 120, 199
residential care settings 61, 101, 104, 114, 118
  see also care homes
respect 32, 34, 60, 98, 102, 103, 116, 156
  for carers 126
  and consent 156
  intimate care 112–14
restriction of independence 125
rights 18, 36, 41, 105, 106–11
  of carers 124
  human rights 107, 109, 156, 181
  medication and 156–60

risk assessments 41–2
    medication 156–8, 161
risk factors for dementia 24
risks 19, 41, 118, 124
    carers' perceptions of 125
    managing 41–2, 96, 110–11
Rogers, Carl, growth-promoting
    climate 32
routes for administration of medication
    149, 150, 154
routines 39, 43, 58, 71, 97, 121
    mealtimes and food 179, 186, 196
    medication 161, 164
safeguarding individuals 18, 31, 41, 67, 105
    legislation for 106–8
safety 33, 105, 122
    of environment 119, 122
    medication and 139, 153–5,
        161, 166
SALT (speech and language therapists)
    27, 72, 196
sedation 143
self-actualisation 34
self-belief 122
self-care 97, 118, 121, 122
self-esteem 34, 43, 89, 120, 121
self-identity 36, 122
self-medication 156, 160, 161
self-neglect 18
self-respect 36, 112, 122
self-worth 103
sense of identity 43
sense of self 31, 60, 62, 88
services for younger people 93
short-term memory loss 11, 13, 20, 23,
    76, 118, 121, 142
side effects 143, 145, 171
    see also adverse reactions to
        medication
sign language 65, 69, 73
signs of dementia 20–3
skills 98
    daily living skills 17, 103, 118,
        119–20
    social skills 54, 76
sleep 99, 183, 202
    medication for 99, 162

smells (food) 190, 199
social changes 57, 58
social environment 17, 58, 120
social model of dementia 17
social needs 34
social relationships 120
social skills 54, 76
social space 115
social workers 71
songs 38, 61, 66
speech and language therapists (SALT)
    27, 72, 196
speech problems 8, 22
statutory services 27–8, 47–8, 49
statutory-voluntary partnerships 47–8
stereotyping 92, 116
stigma 116
stimulating appetite 190, 192
stimulation 37, 38, 41, 89
storage of medication 138, 139, 140,
    145, 154
strengths-based approach 90, 96
stress 92, 181
    mealtimes 192, 193
strokes 22, 57, 114, 183
    mini strokes 22, 126, 141
subcortical dementias 141
supplementary feeding 190–1
supplements (dietary) 146–8
support 27–9, 60
    to achieve potential 118–22
    for carers 44, 49, 108, 123, 124,
        125–7
    for communication 60
    for eating and drinking 196–8,
        200–1
    at home 18, 57, 101
    involving individuals 37–9
    for learning disabled people 96
    minimum level of 103
support plans 73
supporting good nutrition 199–204
supporting the use of medication 161–3
symptoms 8–9, 12–13, 20–3, 26, 93
    treating 16, 17
syringes 151

talking mats 68, 69
techniques for administering medication
    149–52
technologies see assistive technologies
theoretical models of dementia 16–19
time, difficulties with 9, 13
touch 61, 66, 67, 71, 94, 189
traditions 116, 187
transitions 72, 73
triggers 57, 62, 74, 120, 186
tumours, benign 141
types of dementia 20–3
unconditional positive regard 32,
    33, 60
unique individuality 59, 92, 103, 116,
    186, 187
unique needs and preferences 98–101
unused or unwanted medication 154–5
validation therapy 66
valuing people 98, 102–3
    see also devaluation of individual
vascular dementia 20, 22, 25, 192
verbal communication 55–6, 65, 96,
    110, 120
vials 151, 152
visio-spatial perception 179
vision, aids to 11, 71, 74, 75
visual aids 41
visual impairment 11, 26, 75
visual perception 11, 179
voluntary services 29, 47–8, 49
vulnerability 33, 108, 110, 112, 156,
    158, 167
    to illness 180–1
    to neglect and abuse 30–1, 168
wandering 18, 20, 111, 143, 181
weight 195, 202, 202–3
welfare attorneys 107
wellbeing
    indicators 202–3
    promoting 35
withdrawal 9, 58, 65, 126, 179, 183
words, recalling 26
working in the least restrictive way
    110–11
younger people with dementia 92–3

Acknowledgements

Every effort has been made to trace copyright holders and to obtain their permission for the use of copyright material. The publishers will gladly receive any information enabling them to rectify any error or omission at the first opportunity.

The publishers would like to thank the following for permission to reproduce photographs:

(t = top, b = bottom, c = centre, l = left, r = right)

Cover & pi: Stuart Key/Dreamstime.com; pp4–7: Johnny Greig people/Alamy; p8: Wouter van Caspel/iStock; p11: abimages/Shutterstock; p13: Kuzma/Shutterstock; p14: Image Source/Alamy; p16: Rido/Shutterstock; p17: fotoluminate/Shutterstock; p21: Zephyr/Science Photo Library; p24: Goodluz/Shutterstock; p26: Giorgiomtb/ Shutterstock; p29: Paula Solloway/Alamy; p30: Golden Pixels LLC/Shutterstock; p32: Andrew Bassett/Shutterstock; p35: Robert Kneschke/Shutterstock; p37: Monkey Business Images/Shutterstock; p40: Catchlight Visual Services/Alamy; p41: Alexander Raths/Shutterstock; p44: Alexander Raths/Shutterstock; p48: Alina Solovyova-Vincent/iStock; p52–53: Gilles Lougassi/Shutterstock; p56: Kristo-Gothard Hunor/Shutterstock; p59: Paula Solloway/Alamy; p63: Michaela Stejskalova/Shutterstock; p65: Janine Wiedel Photolibrary/Alamy; p68: Galina Zharkova/Shutterstock; p72: imagebroker/Alamy; p74: MBI/Alamy; p76: Mark Bowden/iStock; pp80–83: Catherine Yeulet/iStock; p84: David Young-Wolff/ Alamy; p86: Paul Doyle/Alamy; p89: Mike Abrahams/Alamy; p92: Oleg Golovnev/ Shutterstock; p94: Adrian Sherratt/Alamy; p95: Paula Solloway/Alamy; p96: Luna4/ Shutterstock; p98: Sima/Shutterstock; p99: Paula Solloway/Alamy; p102: Jon Schulte/iStock; p104: Art Directors & TRIP/Alamy; p106: imageegami/Shutterstock; p110: Jaren Jai Wicklund/Shutterstock; p112: Ron Bull/Alamy; p113: Stefanolunardi/ Shutterstock; p115: Larry Lilac/Alamy; p118: Paul Doyle/Alamy; p123: Paula Solloway/Alamy; p127: Yuri Arcurs/Shutterstock; p91: Dean Mitchell/iStock; pp132–135: Mangostock/Shutterstock; p138: Dan White/Alamy; p140: Dinga/ Shutterstock; p143: James Steidl/Shutterstock; p144: Ramona Heim/Shutterstock; p146: Monkey Business Images/Shutterstock; p147: Maskot/Alamy; p150: Olivier Le Queinec/Shutterstock; p151: Arkady/Shutterstock; p152: Kuzma/Shutterstock; p154: Daniel M. Nagy/Shutterstock; p157t: Absolut/Shutterstock; p157b: Creatista/ Shutterstock; p159: Paul Doyle/Alamy; p160: Golden Pixels LLC/Shutterstock; p162: Chris Schmidt/iStock; p163: Penny Tweedie/Alamy; p165: Custom Medical Stock Photo/Alamy; p166: Kacso Sandor/Shutterstock; p167: Yuri Arcurs/Shutterstock; p169: TravelStockCollection - Homer Sykes/Alamy; p171: Jason Stitt/Shutterstock; pp176–177: Monkey Business Images/Shutterstock; p178: David Hoffman/Alamy; p179: Moodboard/Alamy; p182: Simone van den Berg/Shutterstock; p184: Jodi Jacobson/iStock; p187: Blaj Gabriel/Shutterstock; p188: Corbis Flirt/Alamy; p190: Helen Sessions/Alamy; p193: Alexander Raths/iStock; p196: Stockbroker/Alamy; p200: GlowImages/Alamy; p204: Jack Sullivan/Alamy.